SMILE AT FEAR

Smile at Fear

AWAKENING THE TRUE HEART
OF BRAVERY

Chögyam Trungpa

Edited by Carolyn Rose Gimian

Shambhala
Boston & London
2009

Shambhala Publications, Inc.
Horticultural Hall
300 Massachusetts Avenue
Boston, Massachusetts 02115
www.shambhala.com

9 8 7 6 5 4 3 2 1

First edition
Printed in the United States of America

⊗This edition is printed on acid-free paper that meets the American
National Standards Institute Z39.48 Standard.
♻This book was printed on 30% postconsumer recycled paper. For
more information please visit www.shambhala.com.

Distributed in the United States by Random House, Inc.,
and in Canada by Random House of Canada Ltd

Designed by Daniel Urban-Brown

Library of Congress Cataloging-in-Publication Data

Trungpa, Chögyam, 1939–1987.
Smile at fear: awakening the true heart of bravery/Chögyam Trungpa;
edited by Carolyn Rose Gimian.—1st ed.
p.   cm.
Includes index.
ISBN 978-1-59030-696-3 (hardcover: alk. paper)
1. Courage—Religious aspects—Buddhism. 2. Fear—Religious aspects—Buddhism. 3. Religious life—Buddhism. I. Gimian, Carolyn
Rose. II. Title.
BQ4570.C78T78 2009
294.3'5696—dc22
2009010128

WHEN YOU ARE FRIGHTENED by something, you have to relate with fear, explore why you are frightened, and develop some sense of conviction. You can actually look at fear. Then fear ceases to be the dominant situation that is going to defeat you. Fear can be conquered. You can be free from fear, if you realize that fear is not the ogre. You can step on fear, and therefore you can attain what is known as fearlessness. But that requires that, when you see fear, you smile.

—Chögyam Trungpa, *Great Eastern Sun*

Contents

Part Three: Riding the Energy of Windhorse

Editor's Preface

THIS IS A BOOK about all the fears we have, from momentary panic and anxiety, up to the biggest terrors we may face about our life and our death. It is also about the fundamental sources of fear and anxiety, which affect all of us. The author presents practical advice, but not quick fixes. He is trying to help us fundamentally transform our lives and our perceptions so that we can *conquer* fear, not simply suppress it for a time. To become truly fearless, he suggests, we must stop running from our fear and begin to make friends with it. We must learn to smile at fear. This is a critical part of the conquest.

As I write this preface, we are in the midst of a dramatic economic crisis that is creating shock waves of fear and anxiety around the world. It seems a very appropriate time for a book on working with fear. However, given the human condition and the ongoing chaos in the world, it is probably always a good time to look into the issues of fear and fearlessness.

Chögyam Trungpa, one of the greatest Buddhist teachers of the twentieth century, died in 1987. Yet these teachings on spiritual warriorship and bravery seem as though they were written for this very moment in time. He felt that the West, and indeed the world as a whole, would face immense difficulties in the twenty-first century, and he spoke to his students of those potential hardships with a mixture of confidence and realism. Trungpa Rinpoche (Rinpoche is a title for realized teachers that means "Precious One") was sure that humanity could handle what might be coming, but equally sure that the challenges would be substantial. I participated in sobering conversations with him about the economic and political future of North America and other parts of the world.

Rinpoche himself was a man who embodied fearlessness and compassion. In 1950 his homeland of Tibet was invaded by the Chinese Communists, and he was forced to flee the country in 1959 with the knowledge that there was a price on his head. He set off on foot from a remote area in East Tibet to seek refuge in India, leading a group of three hundred Tibetans on a journey that took ten months. Needless to say, they met with extreme challenges and many opportunities to face their fears.

Most of the group was captured in the last months of the journey as they crossed the Brahmaputra River in southern Tibet. Just over fifty of them made it all the way to India. Throughout this journey, Trungpa Rinpoche relied on meditative insight as the basis for his strength and courage, and he never ceased to recommend this approach to others.

After escaping Tibet, sadly, he never saw his mother or any other members of his family again. Yet years later, he expressed his feelings of great compassion for Mao Tse-tung, the revolutionary leader who ordered the invasion of Tibet. In this book he shares the Buddhist teachings that are the basis of this kind of tenderhearted bravery.

Each of us can awaken the same kind of courage in our lives now. What terrifies us doesn't change so much from decade to decade or from one person to another. The fundamental fear we have to work with is the fear of losing ourselves. When the stronghold of ego is threatened, fear is one of our strongest defense mechanisms. Beginning to dismantle it is one of the greatest gifts we can give ourselves or others.

In this volume, Chögyam Trungpa uses the image of the warrior to describe the attitude we can take to invoke fearlessness and bravery in our spiritual practice and in our lives. Rinpoche realized that the secular and the religious would have to be more fully joined in modern spirituality, if spirituality were to truly serve the needs of this time. This is reflected here in his use of the imagery of Shambhala, a mythical country of enlightened citizens ruled by benevolent monarchs. Shambhala is a symbol of the aspiration to build a good society. It also emphasizes the importance of completely engaging with our everyday life. By speaking of the power of the Shambhala world, he is in part pointing to how working with the worldly, ordinary aspects of life can have a transcendent dimension, showing us that the world as it is contains dignity and beauty.

Chögyam Trungpa discusses many levels of working with fear, including how to engage properly with the most extreme situations, such as having to fight an actual enemy, not just an obstacle in your mind. The times we live in seem to call for the kind of gut-level bravery that he exemplified. Having worked with particularly difficult situations in life, he understood real-life challenges. He does not shy away from discussing such situations here. At the same time, he also talks about how each moment can be the opportunity to awaken confidence, through seeing the sacredness of everyday life. This too is a powerful antidote to fear and anxiety. One of the truly remarkable characteristics of his approach is that it steadfastly rejects aggression as a strategy for overcoming obstacles. A deep and powerful well of gentleness is the basis for the bravery of the Shambhala warrior, the practitioner who wants to fully engage life without arrogance or aggression. When we are threatened, it is all too easy to react with anger. When we're hit, we want to hit back. Rinpoche shows us alternatives that are powerful without being destructive. This is wisdom we need.

At the same time, these teachings are not just hard-hitting

but also heartfelt. They emphasize our connection with the heart of the teachings, which we could say is both the heart of the Buddha and the heart of Shambhala. Love is immensely powerful, as we all know. Chögyam Trungpa describes a connection to tenderheartedness and sadness as the energy that powers the development of true human bravery or warriorship, returning to this topic over and over again. Unifying softness and toughness as part of the warrior's path is also a key element. Over and over again, he recommends the discipline of meditation as the key to unlocking this potential.

In the end, this is a book about being genuine, being fully human. If we are willing to be vulnerable, from that vulnerability we can also discover invincibility. Having nothing to lose, we cannot be defeated. Having nothing to fear, we cannot be conquered.

May you enjoy this journey through fear and fearlessness. May it give rise to genuine bravery. May it bring you the smile of fearlessness. May it help to bring peace and prosperity to this world.

Carolyn Rose Gimian
Halifax, Nova Scotia

Part One

THE WAY OF THE WARRIOR

Becoming a warrior and facing yourself is a question of honesty rather than condemning yourself. By looking at yourself, you may find that you've been a bad boy or girl, and you may feel terrible about yourself. Your existence may feel wretched, completely pitch-black, like the black hole of Calcutta. Or you may see something good about yourself. The idea is simply to face the facts. Honesty plays a very important part. Just see the simple, straightforward truth about yourself. When you begin to be honest with yourself, you develop a genuine gut level of truth. That is not necessarily cutting yourself down. Simply discover what is there; simply see that, and then stop! So first, look at yourself, but don't condemn yourself. It's important to be matter-of-fact, on the spot. Just look, and when you see the situation in its fullest way, then you begin to be a warrior.

1

Facing Yourself

OUR SUBJECT MATTER is warriorship. Anyone who is interested in hearing the truth, which in Buddhism we call the dharma; anyone who is interested in finding out about himor herself; and anyone who is interested in practicing meditation is basically a warrior. Many approaches to spirituality and to life in general are influenced by cowardice. If you are afraid of seeing yourself, you may use spirituality or religion as a way of looking at yourself without seeing anything about yourself at all. When people are embarrassed by themselves, there is no fearlessness involved. However, if someone is willing to look at himself or herself, to explore and practice wakefulness on the spot, he or she is a warrior.

"Warrior" here is a translation of the Tibetan word *pawo*. *Pa* means "brave," and *wo* makes it "a person who is brave." The warrior tradition we are discussing is a tradition of bravery. You might have the idea of a warrior as someone who wages war. But in this case, we are not talking about warriors as those who engage in warfare. Warriorship here refers to fundamental bravery and fearlessness.

Warriorship is based on overcoming cowardice and our sense of being wounded. If we feel fundamentally wounded, we may be afraid that somebody is going to put stitches in us to heal our wound. Or maybe we have already had the stitches put in, but we dare not let anyone take them out. The approach of the warrior is to face all those situations of fear or cowardice. The general goal of warriorship is to have no fear. But the ground of warriorship is fear itself. In order to be fearless, first we have to find out what fear is.

Fear is nervousness; fear is anxiety; fear is a sense of inadequacy, a feeling that we may not be able to deal with the challenges of everyday life at all. We feel that life is overwhelming. People may use tranquilizers or yoga to suppress their fear: they just try to float through life. They may take occasional breaks to go to Starbucks or the mall. We have all sorts of gimmicks and gadgets that we use in the hope that we might experience fearlessness simply by taking our minds off of our fear.

Where does fear come from? It comes from basic bewilderment. Where does basic bewilderment come from? It comes from being unable to harmonize or synchronize mind and body. In the sitting practice of meditation, if you have a bad seat on the cushion, you are unable to synchronize your mind and body. You don't have a sense of your place or your posture. This applies to the rest of life as well. When you don't feel grounded or properly seated in your world, you cannot relate to your experience or to the rest of the world.

So the problem begins in a very simple way. When body and mind are unsynchronized, you feel like a caricature of yourself, almost like a primordial idiot or a clown. In that situation, it is very difficult to relate to the rest of the world.

That is a simplified version of what is known as the setting-sun mentality: having completely lost track of the basic harmony of being human. The idea of the setting sun is that the sun is already setting in your world, and you cannot rise above the darkness. You feel that there is only misery, clouds, the dungeon, life in the gutter. To compensate for that, you might go to a very dark dungeon with bad lighting, where you get drunk.

That is called a club. You dance like a drunken ape who has forgotten bananas and its home in the jungle a long time ago. So it feasts on cheap beer while wiggling its tail. There is nothing wrong with dancing per se, but in this case it is a form of escaping from or avoiding your fear. It's very sad. That is the setting sun. It's a dead end, a very dead end.

In contrast to that, the Great Eastern Sun is the sun that is fully risen in your life. It is the sun of wakefulness, the sun of human dignity. It is *Great* because it represents upliftedness and the qualities of openness and gentleness. You have an uplifted sense of posture or place in your world, which we call having good head and shoulders. It is in the *East* because you have a smile on your face. East is the concept of dawn. When you look outside first thing in the morning, you see light coming from the East, even before the sun rises. So the East is the smile you have when you wake up. The sun is about to rise. Fresh air is coming with the dawn. So the sun is in the East and it is Great.

Here, the *Sun* is a completely mature sun, the sun that you see in the sky around ten o'clock in the morning. It is the opposite of the image of the drunken ape dancing at midnight under the light of dim electric bulbs. The contrast is astounding, so extraordinary! The Great Eastern Sun vision is uplifted and awake, fresh and precise.

We could get into further details later, but first we should discuss the fundamental understanding of fear and fearlessness. One of the main obstacles to fearlessness is the habitual patterns that allow us to deceive ourselves. Ordinarily, we don't let ourselves experience ourselves fully. That is to say, we have a fear of facing ourselves. Experiencing the innermost core of their existence is embarrassing to a lot of people. Many people try to find a spiritual path where they do not have to face themselves but where they can still liberate themselves—liberate themselves from themselves, in fact. In truth, that is impossible.

We cannot do that. We have to be honest with ourselves. We have to see our gut, our real shit, our most undesirable parts. We have to see that. That is the foundation of warriorship and the basis of conquering fear. We have to face our fear; we have to look at it, study it, work with it, and practice meditation with it.

We also have to give up the notion of a divine savior, which has nothing to do with what religion we belong to, but refers to the idea of someone or something who will save us without our having to go through any pain. In fact, giving up that kind of false hope is the first step. We have to be with ourselves. We have to be real people. There is no way of beating around the bush, hoping for the best. If you are really interested in working with yourself, you can't lead that kind of double life, adopting ideas, techniques, and concepts of all kinds, simply in order to get away from yourself. That is what we call spiritual materialism: hoping that you can have a nice sleep, under anesthetics, and by the time you awaken, everything will be sewn up. Everything will be healed. In that case, you do not have to go through any pain or problems.

In a genuine spiritual discipline, you cannot do that. You might convince yourself that there is some religious discipline that will allow you to pass directly into spiritual ecstasy. You might convince yourself that this world does not exist; only the realm of the spirit exists. However, later on, something will bounce back on you, because we cannot cheat the basic norm, which is known as karma, or the law of cause and effect. We cannot cheat that.

We have to face quite a lot. We have to give up a lot. You may not want to, but still you have to, if you want to be kind to yourself. It boils down to that. On the other hand, if you want to hurt yourself by indulging in setting-sun neurosis, that is your business and it's nobody else's business. Nobody can save you from yourself. Go ahead. But you are bound to regret it later on, profoundly so. By then, you may have collected so much garbage that it will be almost impossible to undo the situation. That would be a very wretched place to end up.

Often, we prefer to hurt ourselves. It seems to feel better to pursue our habitual patterns than to help ourselves. You may have heard in school that studying hard will be good for you. Your parents may have told you to eat all the food on your plate, because it's good for you. There are a lot of people starving all over the world, and you are fortunate to have this meal in front of you. Eat it up. Maybe such advice is helpful. At the time you heard these things, they may have seemed completely unskillful, in terms of your state of mind. However, such orthodoxy and expression of discipline may have an element of truth in them.

We must decide to look at ourselves and experience ourselves honestly. Some of us find ourselves in the most wretched and profoundly degrading situations. Some of us may have brilliant and good situations happening. Whatever the case may be, whether our exploration brings hope or fear, we look at ourselves. We need to find ourselves, face ourselves, and beyond that, give up our privacy, our inhibition.

There may be a semantic problem here with my use of the word *privacy* in the English language. The point is, that when you give up privacy, that is the only time you can be with yourself. Our normal version of privacy is not really privacy. We say, "I need my privacy." If you are bottling yourself up with your so-called privacy, you find yourself getting in your own way. There is no privacy in that situation. The privacy does not exist. Instead, you feel completely bombarded with internal emotions and thoughts, which take away from your chance to be with yourself and relax with yourself completely. Once you begin to give up privacy, you open your heart and your whole existence to the rest of the world, and then you find greater privacy. You find that an actual discovery of yourself is taking place.

The only way to relax with yourself is to open your heart. Then you have a chance to see who you are. This experience is like opening a parachute. When you jump out of an airplane and open the chute, you are there in the sky by yourself. Sometimes it is very frightening, but on the other hand, when you take this step, the whole situation, the whole journey, makes sense. You have to actually do it, and then you will understand. Giving up privacy is not so much a process of education and logic, but it happens on the spot, by doing so.

One has to give up inhibition, but that does not become exhibitionism. You remain true to yourself if you give up inhibition. You just give up your privacy, your sense of shyness, and the longing to have a personal "trip." When you give that up, it doesn't mean you have to become an exhibitionist; but you could be a real person. When you give up smoking cigarettes, you don't have to proclaim what you have done. Maybe nobody will notice. You just do not smoke anymore. It might be sad for you that nobody can appreciate your virtue, but on the other hand, so what? When you give up your privacy, you still stand and walk on two feet like other human beings. You look at the universe with two eyes, and it is okay, fine. You have become a fully decent human being for the first time, but you do not have to proclaim that. You stop at red lights. You drive when it is green. It's a boring world. One has to take the first step. Then you find that you still maintain the same old standing, which is sometimes terrible, sometimes good, but still standing steady. It is very humorous in some ways, maybe painfully so. Maybe not! In any case, welcome to the warrior's world.

Then you begin to realize that you have something in yourself that is fundamentally, basically good. It transcends the notion of good or bad. Something that is worthwhile, wholesome, and healthy exists in all of us. For the first time, you are seeing the Great Eastern Sun. Goodness arises from discovering the vision of the Great Eastern Sun. This goodness is basic or primordial goodness that you have. You possess it already. Such goodness is synonymous with bravery. It is always there. Whenever you see a bright and beautiful color, you are witnessing your own inherent goodness. Whenever you hear a sweet and beautiful sound, you are hearing your own basic goodness. Whenever you taste something sweet or sour, you are experiencing your own basic goodness. If you are in a room and you open the door and walk outside, there is a sudden breeze of fresh air. Such an experience may last only a second, but that whiff of fresh air is the smell of basic goodness.

Things like that are always happening to you, but you have been ignoring them, thinking that they are mundane and unimportant, purely coincidences of an ordinary nature. However, it is worthwhile to take advantage of anything that happens to you that has that particular nature of goodness. You begin to realize that there is nonaggression happening all around you in your life, and you are able to feel the freshness of realizing your goodness, again and again.

But you can't jump the gun. First, let us look at ourselves. If you put one hundred percent of your heart into facing yourself, then you connect with this unconditional goodness. Whereas, if you only put fifty percent into the situation, you are trying to bargain with the situation, and nothing very much will happen. When you are genuine in the fullest sense, you do not need the conditional judgment of good or bad, but you actually *are* good rather than you *become* good.

If we face ourselves properly, fully, then we find that something else exists there, beyond facing ourselves. Something exists in us that is basically awake, as opposed to asleep. We find something intrinsically cheerful and fundamentally pride-worthy. That is to say, we don't have to con ourselves. We discover genuine one hundred percent gold, not even twenty-four karat. According to the Buddhist tradition, that is discovering our buddha nature. In Sanskrit, buddha nature is *tathagatagarbha*, which means that the essence of the tathagatas, the buddhas who have already gone beyond, exists in us.

We are fundamentally awake. We ourselves are already good. It's not just a potential. It's more than potential. Of course, we will have hesitation again and again in believing that. You might think this goodness is just an old myth, another trick to cheer us up. But no! It is real and good. Buddha nature exists in us, and because of that, we are here. Your basic buddha nature brought you here.

The heart of the matter, the technique that seems to be the only way to realize this, is the sitting practice of meditation. Meditation is the key to seeing yourself as well as to seeing beyond yourself. Seeing yourself is the first aspect, discovering all sorts of terrible things going on in you. Facing the possibilities and the realities of that is not all that bad. If you begin to do that, you are being an honest person. Then, beyond that, you have to have further vision. Your honesty allows you to realize your goodness. You do possess Buddha in your heart.

2

Meditation: Touch and Go

ONCE WE BEGIN TO ACKNOWLEDGE that goodness exists within us, it is necessary to go beyond our doubts and adopt the attitude that we are worthy people and we have something going for us. We are not totally wretched. We have to go through the clouds, but then we see the sun. This basic approach to discovering the worthiness of our existence is the warrior's philosophy of looking at ourselves.

How do we get to this point? What is the technique for discovering ourselves in both ways, the negative and the positive? How can we do that? Should we put our mind in a machine or under a microscope to study ourselves? Should we discover ourselves by doing Outward Bound or by swimming in the ocean or lying on the beach?

There are all sorts of possibilities, obviously. However, there is really only one way to do this. The only way is to be with yourself for a long period of time, spending lots of seconds, minutes, and hours with yourself. We have never done this properly and fully at all. We may try to be with ourselves by reading a magazine, watching television, drinking beer, smoking all sorts of things, popping pills, having a chat with a friend, or taking a rest in bed. But we have not been with ourselves fully, properly. We always try to *do something* with ourselves, rather than simply *be* with ourselves. If you cannot *be* with yourself, you cannot find

11

out who you are or where you are. In that case, the essence of what you are is impossible to find.

There is something further, which is also to find out how you are *not*, why you are not, where you are not. The essence of this discovery is that you are actually nonexistent. By trying to find out who you are, you might find out that you are not anything at all. Then, although you find out that you are *not*, you discover there is still some glowing brilliance that exists within the experience of nonexistence.

The recommended technique to be with ourselves fully is the practice of meditation. In the sitting practice of meditation, we are not applying old methods to a new world, but we are simply learning to lead our lives fully. This style of meditation was particularly recommended by Shakyamuni Buddha himself, and it is the way in which I myself was trained. It has been known as the best technique for beginning meditators for more than twenty-five hundred years.

I personally have learned from applying this approach to meditation. This is not offered as some kind of testimonial, but I actually have gained wisdom and clarity myself from practicing in this way. I have gone through exactly the same basic training and discipline that I'm presenting to you. (The only difference is that you are not hearing the teachings in Tibetan!)

Cultivating mindfulness is the attitude that allows us to see ourselves and our world quite accurately and precisely. When we talk about *attitude* in this context, we are talking about developing the awareness of mind, which is precisely what mindfulness is. Awareness of mind means that you are fundamentally aware and that your mind is aware of yourself. In other words, you're aware that you're aware. You are not a machine; you are an individual person relating with what's happening around you. Mindfulness is developing this sense of being.

To describe meditation, we could use the phrase *touch and go*.

You are in contact, you're touching the experience of being there, actually being there, and then you let go. That applies to awareness of your breath on the cushion and also beyond that to your day-to-day living awareness. The point of *touch and go* is that there is a feeling of being yourself fully and truly. The point of *touch* is that there is a sense of existence, that you are who you are.

When you sit on the cushion, you know and you feel that you are sitting on the cushion and that you actually exist. You are there, you are sitting, you are there, you are sitting. That's the *touch* part. The *go* part is that you are there, and then you don't hang on to it. You don't sustain your sense of being, but you let go of even that. Touch and go.

When you meditate, it is recommended that you sit cross-legged on a meditation cushion, as opposed to hanging out in any convenient posture. In any case, you sit properly, whether you sit on a cushion or, if you are unable to sit on the ground, you sit in a chair. You have a straight spine, your breath is not strained, and your neck doesn't have any strain on it. So sit, upright. If necessary, you can change your posture and rearrange yourself. There's no point in punishing yourself.

This is a difference between animals and human beings. Some animals find relaxation while they are still standing, with their spines horizontal to the ground. Horses sometimes sleep that way. They could even meditate that way, if anybody taught horses to meditate. Snakes and lizards and horses and cows could meditate with their bodies horizontal to the ground. But as far as human beings are concerned, we don't walk on four feet at this point in our evolution. We have no chance of going back, so we have to walk on our two feet. For us, a vertical posture is natural, including when we meditate. So since we are formed this way, we should do it this way. The Buddha, setting an example for human beings, sits upright in the meditation posture. This isn't particularly anthropocentric in the sense that human beings are regarded as the highest beings. It's a question of what our makeup is, and we should go along with our makeup. So posture is very important. It's upright as opposed to animal style, and not too tense in your neck. Just sit up, very simply.

When you sit up properly, you are there. Your breathing follows naturally. I've noticed that when people see something interesting happening in a movie, everybody sits up in perfect posture. So that's an example for us. It is happening, it is your life, and you are upright, and you are breathing. Practice is very personal and direct.

The attitude toward the breath in meditation is to become the breathing. Try to identify completely rather than watching your breath or just observing the process of breathing. You are the breath; the breath is you. Breath is coming out of your nostrils, going out and dissolving into the atmosphere, into the space. You put a certain energy and effort toward your awareness of that. Then, as for in-breathing, should you try to deliberately draw things in? That's not recommended here. Just boycott your breath; boycott your concentration on the breath. As your breath goes out, let it dissolve. Just abandon it, boycott it.

So breathing in is just space. Physically, biologically, one does breathe in, obviously, but that's not a big deal and you don't emphasize it. Then another breath goes out—be with it. So it's: out, dissolve, gap; out, dissolve, gap. It is a constant process: opening, gap, abandoning, boycotting. Boycotting, in this case, is a very significant word. If you hold on to your breath, you are holding on to yourself constantly. Once you begin to boycott the end of the out-breath, then there's no world left, except that the next out-breath reminds you to tune in. So you tune in, dissolve, tune in, dissolve, tune in, dissolve.

Thoughts arise in the midst of practice: "Where should I take yoga?" "When can I write another article?" "What's happening with my investments?" "I hate so-and-so, who was so terrible to me," "I would love to be with her," and "What's the story with my parents?" All kinds of thoughts arise naturally. If you have lots of time to sit, endless thoughts happen constantly.

The approach to that is actually no approach. Reduce everything to the thought level—recognize that all of this is just thinking. Usually, if you have mental chatter, you call it your thoughts. But if you have deeply involved emotional chatter, you give it special prestige. You think those thoughts deserve the special privilege of being called *emotion*. Somehow, in the realm of actual mind, things don't work that way. Whatever arises is just thinking: thinking you're horny, thinking you're angry. As far as meditation practice is concerned, your thoughts are no longer regarded as VIPs, while you meditate. You think, you sit; you think, you sit; you think, you sit. You have thoughts, you have thoughts about thoughts. Let it happen that way. Call them thoughts.

Then, there is a further *touch* that is necessary. Emotional states should not be just acknowledged and pushed off, but actually looked at. During meditation you may experience being utterly aggressive and angry, or being utterly lustful, whatever. You don't just say to your emotion, very politely, "Hi. Nice seeing you again. You are okay. Good-bye, I want to get back to my breath." That's like meeting an old friend who reminds you of the past, and rather than stopping to talk, you say, "Excuse me, I don't have time to talk. I have to catch the train to my next appointment." In this approach to practice, you don't just sign off. You acknowledge what's happening, and then you look more closely as well.

You don't give yourself an easy time to escape the embarrassing and unpleasant moments, the self-conscious moments of your life. Such thoughts might arise as memories of the past, the painful experience of the present, or painful future prospects. All those things happen, and you experience them and

15

look at them, and only then do you come back to your breath. This is very important.

If you feel that sitting and meditating is a way of avoiding problems, then that is the problem itself. In fact, most of the problems in life don't come from being an aggressive or lustful person. The greatest problem is that you want to bottle those things up and put them aside, and you become an expert in deception. That is one of the biggest problems. Meditation practice should uncover any attempts to develop a subtle, sophisticated, deceptive approach.

In meditation, there is a sense of individuality, a sense of person. Actually, we are here, we exist. What about the nonexistence and egolessness that Buddhism emphasizes? What about spiritual materialism, wanting happiness and fulfillment from our practice? Aren't we going to stray into some kind of pitfall? Maybe you are. Maybe you are not. There's no guarantee, since there's no guarantor. However, it is possible that you could just do this technique very simply. I would recommend that you not worry about future security, but just do this, directly, simply.

Our attitude when we finish meditating is also very important. We should even out our whole experience of life and have a good time throughout life. Meditating is not like being in prison, and the rest of life is not vacation or freedom. Everything should be included. That seems to be the basic meditative approach to life. Whether you sit or you stand, it's the same thing; whether you eat or sleep, it's the same. It's the same good old world. You carry your world with you in any case; you can't cut your world into different slices and put them into different pigeonholes.

We don't have to be so poverty-stricken about our life. We don't have to try to get a little chocolate chip from one corner of our life. "All the rest of life may be sour, but here in this corner I can take a dip in pleasure." If your body is hot and you dip your finger in ice water, it might feel good, but it's also painful, not particularly pleasurable. If you really know the meaning of pleasure in the total sense, a dip in pleasure is just further punishment and an unnecessary trick that we play on ourselves. From that point of view, the practice of meditation is not so much about the hypothetical attainment of enlightenment. It is about leading a good life. In order to learn how to lead a good life, a spotless life, we need continual awareness that relates with life constantly, directly, very simply.

3

The Moon in Your Heart

BECOMING A WARRIOR and facing yourself is a question of honesty rather than condemning yourself. By looking at yourself, you may find that you've been a bad boy or girl, and you may feel terrible about yourself. Your existence may feel wretched, completely pitch-black, like the black hole of Calcutta. Or you may see something good about yourself. The idea is simply to face the facts. Honesty plays a very important part. Just see the simple, straightforward truth about yourself. When you begin to be honest with yourself, you develop a genuine gut level of truth. That is not necessarily cutting yourself down. Simply discover what is there; simply see that, and then stop! So first, look at yourself, but don't condemn yourself. It's important to be matter-of-fact, on the spot. Just look, and when you see the situation in its fullest way, then you begin to be a warrior.

When you acknowledge that you feel so wretched, you can be fully cheerful. That is the interesting twist. You are being a wholesome, honest person. Usually, we aren't this honest. You may think you can cheat the universe, and out of that, you develop all sorts of naughty or neurotic potentialities, convincing yourself that you do not have to look into your situation honestly. However, when you are just there, then, if you see the actual darkness, that will inspire light or sunrise.

You begin to find that you are a genuine person. You begin to feel good and solid, and beyond that, more than solid, more than real, you realize that you have guts of some kind. Buddha nature is in you already, because you are so true to yourself, true in the sense of being unconditionally honest. In fact, there is no such thing as the true self, the solidly *real* self. When you see yourself genuinely, you find that the concept of reality actually starts to fade. Instead, you find a very large space there, which is unconditional and contains ventilation and breathing space. When you have seen yourself fully, you begin to feel unconditionally good.

At the same time, you begin to acknowledge the existence of greater wisdom. You realize that actually, no matter how smart or learned you may be, you don't know very much about the nature of reality. You need help to make a genuine connection with yourself. Someone has to help you to wake up. For some people, it's enough to encounter this wakefulness or wisdom in a book or in the form of a contemplative discipline that you practice. Nevertheless, it comes from somewhere. Originally, wisdom had to come from a human being's inspiration and understanding, which he or she was willing to share. We are quite fortunate if we encounter a genuine teacher, a human being who shares their knowledge and wisdom directly with us, perhaps by teaching us to meditate or in other ways.

In the Buddhist tradition, when we make a genuine connection with ourselves, we also begin to respect the source of wisdom, the teacher. A genuine teacher has her own awe and respect for knowledge. Our relationship with that person is based on acknowledging her superior comprehension. So our appreciation of the teacher relates to her comprehension rather than to her rank. Our relationship and our respect are from the point of view of respecting the knowledge and the holder of the knowledge. Somebody who has more information than we do about the nature of reality is worthy of respect.

Relating with a teacher is not just a one-way situation. There has to be communication both from the teacher to the student and from the student to the teacher. As our relationship with a teacher develops, at a certain point the teacher may become what is known as a spiritual friend. Such a spiritual friend is an honest friend, a direct friend, a genuine friend, a friend who has developed enough power and strength to actually help others.

We begin to realize that the teacher is not just an information booth or spiritual encyclopedia. The genuine teacher has developed a certain kind of power, which expresses her connection to the phenomenal world. We are not talking about magical power. Rather, we are talking about the strength that comes from connecting with reality, which is much more powerful than any fantasy. As a result of her own training, the teacher develops the power to share or transmit that realization or sanity to others. That transmission takes place through communication between teacher and student and through their development of a basic understanding of each other, to begin with. It has to be an organic relationship. The spiritual friend has no hesitation in telling you the truth and in minding your business. And when the time is right, at the appropriate moment, an authentic spiritual friend can awaken the heart of enlightenment in your system. You become aware of the heart of buddha (which has been there all the time) as though it is entering your heart, just like medicine injected into your veins.

Obviously, there will be resistance to allowing someone to come into your world and inject something into your existence. It could be very unsettling. This technique was not brewed up yesterday or today. It has been happening for more than two thousand five hundred years on this earth. It has been done thousands even millions of times, and it has succeeded thousands and millions of times.

When that particular element, which is your buddha nature, is awakened in your being, strangely enough you think it is a foreign element in your system. According to the Buddhist tradition, this experience is known as transplanting the heart of enlightenment, or transplanting the full moon into your heart. It might be easier to understand if we speak of sharing or awakening, rather than transplanting the full moon, which helps us to realize that although we are receiving the moon as a gift, in fact it is already there within us.

Imagine the full moon coming through your living-room window, coming closer and closer and suddenly entering your heart. You might be freaked out or resent the whole thing, but usually it is a tremendous relief. "Phew, the full moon has entered my heart." It's great, wonderful in fact.

On the other hand, when the full moon comes into your heart, you might have a little panic. "Good heavens, what have I done? There's a moon in my heart. What am I going to do with it? It is too shiny." You might panic much more than if you discovered you were pregnant. When the baby is born, it is going to be tiny. It's not going to come out and start minding your business right away. It has to learn to breathe, suckle, walk, and talk. It has to be toilet trained. But this moon is fully developed. It may have just entered your heart this morning, but it's fully, totally there. That's it! We have absolutely no choice. So we might be somewhat fearful. The mind of the ego may feel that it's been deflowered. You have lost your stronghold.

We are used to calling ourselves "I" and speaking of "my" or "mine." "I would never let anybody into my world. My self is *my* self." Now that toughness known as aggression has been overcome. The moon has been transplanted into your heart, and you may not like it. Sometimes it feels terrible. "What have I done?" You hope it's just a dream, another phase. Unfortunately, it turns out not to be a phase or a trial run, but it is real, absolutely real. We have planted the full moon of enlightenment in our heart. By the way, that moon cannot wane. It never wanes; it is always waxing.

In the process of realizing that, we may also begin to feel very sad. We have lost the virginity of our ego, fundamentally speaking. We might feel somewhat good, but at the same time we feel a sense of loss. We want to hang on to our good old ego. Good old Joe Schmidt or Susie Doe used to be full of ego and used to have tremendous courage, flair, and aggression. We used to take tremendous pride in our jealousy, and we never experienced defeat. We used to do just fine. If people got in our way, we used to get rid of them one way or another. But now life is a mess. We let that silly moon come into our heart. We became softened and saddened, and we cannot carry out our machismo anymore.

In extreme cases, you might want to destroy anything connected with that principle of wakefulness. You might think about assassinating your teacher, burning your books, and, if necessary, destroying yourself, to get away from the moon. You think it could drive you crazy.

On the other hand, if you look at this from an unconditional view, this is the greatest breakthrough that you could ever have in your life. If you really look at the moon in your heart, you feel so good. It is the first step. For the first time, you have discovered yourself as a real person, as opposed to being a fake. Still, you remain somewhat lonely and sad. Such sadness is longing for higher wisdom and further discovery. There is more to come.

4

The Sun in Your Head

HAVING AWAKENED the moon in your heart, you feel a sense of aloneness and natural heartache. Loneliness may be your resistance to going forward, a sign of holding back. Having the moon in your heart, you don't want to be hassled by further moons, other human beings. It feels good to be self-contained, and you hesitate to go beyond that. At that point, further heroism, or warriorship, is very much needed.

The next step is the acceptance of magic. We are not talking about changing water into fire or walking on the ceiling. By referring to magic here, we are saying that we can transform our experience of the phenomenal world. Our normal experiences of passion, aggression, and ignorance can be transformed into a natural state of existence, a state free from passion, free from aggression, and free from ignorance. Such an experience of natural magic comes from transplanting the sun into ourselves.

According to the Buddhist tradition, the sun represents feminine principle and the moon is regarded as masculine principle. The feminine principle is connected with giving birth and providing growth and fertility. Where do you transplant the sun? You might find this rather surprising, but the sun is transplanted into your brain, inside your head. The moon, the masculine principle, was planted in your heart, but the sun is planted in your brain.

What are the qualities of the sun? It contains natural wakefulness as well as fearlessness and gentleness. We use the word *natural* to describe this state of being to contrast it with anything that is manufactured. If something is manufactured, it is artificial, obviously. Here, natural wakefulness refers to a state of being without any struggle or aggression involved. So the sun represents ongoing gentleness and graciousness, as well as fearlessness. All of those principles are transplanted into your head.

When the sun, the feminine principle, is transplanted or awakened in your brain, you see the need to organize your life to reflect this natural state of intelligence or discrimination. You would like your world to be somewhat neat and tidy, and beyond that, it could become glorious and handsome. So you begin to transform your world into a palace of sorts, a palace of accommodation and elegance. Such an elegant environment is not modeled on *House Beautiful* or *Architectural Digest*. The feeling is closer to Genghis Khan's court, shockingly enough. This has nothing to do with Asian culture or the martial arts, particularly, but rather with evoking a natural sense of dignity and splendor.

I worked with an architect when we were building an addition to Karmê-Chöling, a practice center I founded with my students in rural Vermont. This gentleman planned the whole addition, from the shrine room to renovating the kitchen. We agreed about everything until I suggested that we needed columns in the shrine hall. He couldn't understand that at all. He came up with myriad reasons why we shouldn't put columns in the middle of the hall. He thought it would destroy the visual appeal of the room, and that it might actually create architectural problems. He almost was suggesting that the building would collapse if we put columns in the room. We talked and talked and talked. Finally, he begrudgingly agreed to the columns, but he still couldn't understand why I wanted them. Later, when the engineers reviewed the plans, it turned out that there was a structural need for the columns. The architect thought they were just ornamentation, but they turned out to have a function, and he did a *big* double take. This is an example of how the principle of the sun operates in your head.

The sun in your head brings natural intelligence to how you organize your world. A building has to have windows and doors, and beams and even columns—if necessary. Your life requires structure as well. This sense of organization is more fundamental than putting carpet on the floor or whitewashing your walls. A sense of protection, or the quality of having a container, is needed in your life. That sense of a perimeter or container, as well as finding the natural exit and entrance that exist in your world, comes from the sun that you have transplanted into your head. You begin to see how the intelligence shines forth in the space, because the brilliance of warriorship has developed.

You need more than an empty structure to express wakefulness in your life. Who will inhabit the space? We are talking about creating a wakeful atmosphere in your life. Individuals create the atmosphere. Someone holds the posture or the function of a window in a situation, letting in light or ventilating the space. Someone else becomes the door, or the entrance; another individual becomes the pillar that is holding up or reinforcing the space; and another person becomes the kitchen sink, the practicality in the situation. It's not enough to have inanimate objects creating the arrangement of space. Individuals have to become the ceiling, windows, and walls. That is the essence of natural existence, which we call the mandala principle.

There should be dignity and honesty in the environment. With the sun in your head, those qualities are the reference points for arranging our world. Many people have never experienced dignity and honesty put together. People may think that dignity is pompous or fake, very different from the ruggedness of honesty. They think that honesty is like throwing up, regurgitating everything and not holding anything back. But there's another kind of honesty, in which we can be dignified and humble people. That is the essence of the warrior's decorum.

The honesty and trustworthiness of the environment speaks for itself. If someone has been suspicious of what you're doing, when they come into an environment that you've created and they can see your vision actualized, they might begin to relax and accept you. When you transplant the sun of wisdom in your head, there is wakefulness, there is a natural sense of existence, and there is genuineness, all at the same time. It is quite a cheerful world, extraordinarily delightful.

5

Indestructible Nature

WARRIORSHIP IS A NATURAL process of growth. Having developed a basic understanding and connection to warriorship, we plant the moon in our heart, which contains gentleness, compassion, and wakefulness. Then we plant the sun in our head, which brings further wakefulness and genuineness into the whole situation.

The growth of warriorship comes from an absence of laziness. We are generally quite lazy about making a spiritual journey in life. Laziness here is simply that we can't be bothered. You might be vaguely interested in becoming a more developed person, but you're too lazy to do so. Having overcome that attitude, then you can transplant the moon in your heart, which is connected with developing your giving, compassionate nature. You develop kindness and gentleness, or maitri, in yourself, and beyond that you develop compassion, or karuna.

Planting the sun in your head is connected with the development of further intellect, or prajna. Sometimes we resist the idea of developing our intellect. Intellectualization has a bad connotation. We associate it with distancing ourselves from our feelings, refusing to look at ourselves or examine ourselves in a fundamental way. However, using our intellect to understand life is actually quite good. Intellect, or prajna, represents the sharpest point in our experience. Sharpening our intellect brings precision. Intellect brings a direct way of seeing things as they are, so that we don't neglect the potential in our experience. Prajna teaches us to be aware and precise on the spot.

Then we can separate our experiences into the samsaric or confused ones and the enlightened or wakeful ones. In the sitting practice of meditation, we are able to discriminate between what are discursive thoughts and what is the essence of mindfulness and awareness. We begin to realize there are differences between the two. However, neither of them is rejected or accepted per se. We include everything in our practice. Our world of practice does not have to be stingy, but it becomes highly intelligent.

If we understand how to go about things in our own life already, then we will develop a natural sense of how to extend out to others as well. That ability to reach out is based first on how one actually views oneself as Joe Schmidt or Karen Doe. Is this a good Joe Schmidt? Is this a wretched Karen Doe? Or is this David Doe questionable? It is possible, and it has been done in the past, to take an attitude toward oneself that is quite positive and ordinary, in some sense, but which is also extraordinary and which sees life as worthy of celebrating. We can cheer up our attitude toward ourselves. Joe Schmidt could feel a genuine sense of Joe-Schmidt-ness in himself. There is an actual connection that we could make with ourselves.

In some sense, that's very tricky. If you are trying to attain Joe-Schmidt-hood, egohood, it is problematic. Joe-Schmidt-hood is stubborn, aggressive, and speedy. On the other hand, Joe-Schmidt-*ness* is quite reasonable; such a Joe Schmidt is not looking to attain Joe-Schmidt-*hood* at all, but rather a could-not-care-less existence. That Joe has planted the sun in his head. That Joe Schmidt has a natural sense of dignity. At that point, Joe Schmidt or Karen Doe has achieved some genuine understanding of him- or herself. It may not be a full-blown accomplishment, but at that point, Joe and Karen begin to relax and feel good about themselves.

Step by step, the situation evolves and becomes cheerful and humorous at the same time. Karen and Joe develop industriousness. They enjoy life; they eat good food; they enjoy how they dress, how they walk, how they talk, how they live. Although they might be living in just one room, their living situation can be uplifted and elegant. Having lots of money and a big apartment doesn't solve your problems. You still experience emotional struggles of all kinds. The point is that, whatever your environment is, you can create an uplifted living situation. In the warrior's world, you are the king or queen of your domain, in your own right. This sense of celebration comes from joining the moon in your heart and the sun in your head. Elegance and dignity become natural and lovely, wholesome and good. There is no deceit and no pretense of any kind.

This natural wholesomeness is the beginning of developing what we call vajra or indestructible nature. *Vajra* is a Sanskrit word; it is *dorje* in Tibetan. There is really no good English translation that I have found. *Vajra* means having a diamond-like nature, a nature that is indestructible. Having developed some elegance in our own personal existence, which is reflected in our sense of demeanor and composure, we then discover something further, which is known as vajra nature. It is a quality of indestructible wakefulness and undeniable presence.

The indestructibility of vajra nature is the idea that nobody can talk you out of your commitment or your existence. Nobody can actually challenge your realization of warriorship at all. The perimeter has been covered; therefore there is no chance that intruders will get in. You cannot get inside a diamond. The diamond is completely a diamond already, completely indestructible and unassailable. You might think that if you begin to develop such a vajra existence, you might become too proud, too arrogant, and you might try to build up your own egocentrism. That is possible in theory, but in practice, if a

31

person has actually planted the moon in his or her heart, that is already giving up one's individual reality or egotism.

Without the practice of meditation, it is difficult if not impossible to achieve this understanding. Even though you may have only ten minutes a day in your schedule to practice, it is worthwhile to meditate for those ten minutes. It will help you to discover gentleness and goodness in your life, and it will help you to organize your life properly, so that you can actually appreciate the moon in your heart and the sun in your head and develop vajra nature as well.

Vajra nature is associated with enlightened warriorship. It refers to uncovering the warrior's basic being. The word *warrior* is a neutral term, as we have said. It does not particularly refer to either a man or a woman. If we said "warriorette" or "warrioress" to refer to a woman warrior, that would diminish the sense of feminine warriorship altogether. So we just use the term *warrior*.

The feminine principle is very powerful, according to the Shambhala principles of nonaggressive warriorship, as well as the Buddhist principles of nonaggression. When you must engage or attack an enemy, an obstacle, the best attack is based on employing the power of the feminine principle. One of the most lethal weapons arises when the feminine principle turns into wrath. The symbolism of arrowheads, exploding bombs, the tip of a whip, and tongues of flame is all based on the feminine principle, a touch of femininity, which is deadly.

The masculine principle is actually very quiet and gentle, just like the moon. Consider a torch, for instance. The masculine principle provides the handle for the flame. The stick you hold in your hand is the masculine principle, which is solid, reliable comradeship. On top of that burns the feminine flame, which is unpredictable or perhaps untrustworthy in this sense. You cannot take it for granted.

The feminine principle fulfills actions at the same time. If you study a sword with a blade on only one side, the feminine principle is associated with the sharp blade or the cutting process. The masculine principle provides the weight behind the blade. The blade is regarded as the feminine principle, which actually cuts through the situation. It can produce blood, and it creates birth and death. In the case of a sword, it can cause death. The thick metal behind the blade provides weight, which is a sense of loyalty and connectedness. In some traditions, the moon is regarded as feminine and the sun is masculine, but here it is the opposite. If you look at your experience and how we relate with one another, I think you'll find this way of seeing is far more accurate.

What connects or joins the sun and the moon together is the genuineness or straightforward truthfulness of vajra nature. The two principles have to be joined together without deception. To make a good sword, the sharp blade and the weight of the sword must be merged. If you handle a samurai sword, you will feel how it is light and heavy at the same time. Vajra nature is how we can join our experience together to manifest ourselves in the world. It is the diamond-like manifestation of buddha nature. It is putting buddha nature into practice.

6

Sacred World

THE EXPERIENCE OF SACREDNESS brings together the moon in your heart and the sun in your head, as well as supporting the basic sense of sanity or vajra nature in your existence. As we have been discussing, we often have a wretched and small notion of our lives. We try to be good boys and girls. We struggle through life, making our journey stitch by stitch, day by day. We struggle through the day, we go to sleep, we get up the next day, and we do it all over again, without much sense of inspiration. That approach to life is often depressed and undignified, small and flat, like flat Coca-Cola. Sometimes something exciting happens and we feel a little better for a while. We cheer up and we feel pretty good. But behind that, there is the same familiar depressing "me" haunting us all the time.

The wretched familiar "me" is like a lead shoe that weights us down. However, we don't actually have to live that way at all. We could have a sense of celebration and positive arrogance. It's not that we should abandon one part of ourselves and cultivate the other part, but we could simply look at our Joe-Schmidt-ness, the you-ness, with openness. When we do that, there is space to fall in love with ourselves, in the positive sense. You begin to like Joe Schmidt, and at that point, the other wretched Joe begins to phase out. It's not that your personality has changed, particularly, but rather that the positive aspect of yourself has expanded. We could see our world as a big world and see ourselves as open and vast. We can see our world as sacred, which is the key to bringing together the sun and moon.

Sacredness comes from developing gentleness toward ourselves. Then the irritation of being with oneself is taken away. When that kind of friendliness to oneself occurs, then one also develops friendliness toward the rest of the world. At that point, sadness, loneliness, and wretchedness begin to dissipate. We develop a sense of humor. We don't get so pissed off if we have a bad cup of coffee in the morning. Appreciating our human dignity comes from that, and then the moon in your heart becomes natural and obvious, and the sun in your head is also obvious and natural.

Sacredness is not trying to look on the bright side of life and using that as a stepping-stone, but it is unconditional cheerfulness that has no other side. It is just one side, one taste. From that, goodness begins to dawn in your heart. Therefore, whatever we experience, whatever we see, whatever we hear, whatever we think—all these activities have a sense of holiness or sacredness in them. The world is full of hospitality at that point. Sharp corners begin to dissolve, and the darkness begins to lift in our lives.

This is not too good to be true. Such goodness and sacredness are unconditionally good. At the point of realizing this, we become decent human beings and real warriors. We need to remind ourselves over and over that this approach always has to be accompanied by the sitting practice of meditation. Meditation acts as a training ground, a stronghold, and out of that, the seed of friendliness to oneself is planted. The main point is to appreciate our world, which becomes the vajra world, the warrior's world, which is a cheerful world. It never becomes too good or too bad.

For a true warrior, the basic notion of victory is not one-upmanship over your enemy. Victory is unconditional victory, based on unconditional warriorship. Sacredness means that fearlessness is carried out throughout everyday life situations, including brushing your teeth and washing the dishes. Fearlessness takes place all over the place, all the time.

In the setting-sun or confused world, discipline and uniformity have been abused quite a lot. But acting with discipline and maintaining some uniformity does not have to be aggressive. Uniformity in the warrior's world can be a powerful vehicle for us to achieve one mind. That one mind is the mind of gentleness. The warrior's discipline is not an expression of aggression, but it is guarding against one's own aggression. So warriors should be very gentle, and not only gentle but resourceful, awake, and good human beings.

For a warrior, whatever you wear is a uniform, in some sense. If you have two arms and two eyes and one nose, that is your uniform. Everybody has it! The artificial uniforms that are put on top of that in the setting-sun world are often an expression of aggression, obviously. But in the warrior's world, some uniformity is an expression of confidence and gentleness.

Unconditional fearlessness is cheerful and very light. There is no need for any kind of cowardice or fear, or any moments of doubt. It might actually be better to speak of being doubtless rather than fearless. For the warrior, there is no doubt; there are no second thoughts about anything. Because the world is complete, as it is, there is no room for doubt. So the real notion of victory is not having to deal with an enemy at all.

If victory is the notion of no enemy, then the whole world is a friend. That seems to be the warrior's philosophy. The true warrior is not like a person carrying a sword and looking behind his own shadow, in case somebody is lurking there. That is the setting-sun warrior's point of view, which is an expression of cowardice. The true warrior always has a weapon, in any case. Many things in your life function as a weapon, a vehicle for communication that cuts through aggression. It could be anything. It you are wearing a mustache, that could be your weapon. It's not necessary for the warrior to carry an artificial weapon, like a gun. Cowardly people carry guns because they are so cowardly, so afraid. One doesn't have to be afraid of touching a weapon, such as a gun, or even using it when necessary, but that doesn't mean you have to carry one all the time. The definition of warriorship is fearlessness and gentleness. Those are your weapons. The genuine warrior becomes truly gentle because there is no enemy at all.

7

The Education of the Warrior

IN THIS CHAPTER, we will look at the education of the warrior to help us to tune in to the warrior tradition altogether.
This gives us another view of working with fearful mind so that
we can awaken the warrior discipline in ourselves and have a
clear vision of the Great Eastern Sun, the sun of wakefulness.
We must make a personal journey through the warrior principles, and that journey is based on our personal psychological
development or processing. When we describe the education
of the warrior here, it is a way of reflecting on what we have accomplished on our own path, as well as providing inspiration
for how to work with others.

To begin with, we have fearful mind. That fearful mind is the
mentality of those who are still taking pleasure in hibernating in
the cocoon of comfort. People come up with long lists of reasons
they would like to hibernate. They complain that the world has
not provided enough hospitality, so therefore they have to stay
in their cocoons. Philosophers, psychologists, musicians, math-
ematicians, cooks, and seamstresses alike—all kinds of people
with all kinds of mentalities—may have their own answers as to
why they should be left in their own particular cocoons.

Based on that situation of fear, the baby or infant warriors,
would-be warriors, may have arguments or logics to justify remaining in their cocoons. Those of us who have left the cocoon

- and joined the warrior's world always treat such would-be warriors gently. We respect them, but on the other hand, we don't just let them lie in their cocoons forever. We gently take the cocooners out of their cocoons and we place them, instead, in the cradle of loving-kindness, hoping that they will not be bothered by being disturbed.

Sometimes they are offended. They might cry and kick and even shoot a jet of diarrhea right in our face, but they are still somewhat feeble and sweet. In spite of their kicking and screaming, we place them in the cradle of loving-kindness. We take pride in such persons and regard them as would-be warriors, in spite of all their bad temper. We are not put off. Nevertheless, the first step, providing loving care and loving-kindness, takes lots of patience.

Having settled them in the cradle, then we provide them with the profound and brilliant milk that comes from doubtlessness. Doubtlessness is the style in which we feed these cocooners. The milk is profound and brilliant because it is not ordinary milk but comes from the blessings of the warrior lineage. So this milk does not just nourish their cocoon-ness so that one day they can return to their cocoons. This is special milk, right from the breast of the feminine principle, which here represents the peace and harmony of the Shambhala world. It's excellent milk.

Drinking this milk, the cocooners begin to evolve further. However, we shouldn't be too naive in our expectations. They might still kick and scream at the top of their lungs, but it is good exercise that develops them further. They should have good lungs; they should have good muscles. So we let them kick and scream. As long as they get this profound and brilliant milk, that's the best thing they could have at this stage.

Then, in the atmosphere of fearlessness, the cool shade of fearlessness, you wave the fan of joy and happiness. You don't want to overfeed the cocooners with this thick and sweet milk or let them stay completely enveloped in their small domestic situation, constantly drinking milk. You want them to experience some sense of the bigger atmosphere at this point. The educational process is designed so that they will step out of the crib, the cradle, sooner or later, so to help prepare them for that, in the atmosphere of fearlessness, you wave the fan of delight, joy, and happiness. They can go out a little bit, at least into the backyard or the garden. They are being introduced to the world outside, which in this case is just the shade of fearlessness. It's not the greatest step, but it's better than being cooped up in their little homes all the time.

At this point the cocooner rides in a baby carriage or a stroller. It's grown quite strong in the cradle from kicking, but it still has to be driven around in a carriage. Nevertheless, you can take it to witness all kinds of situations, all kinds of shows of phenomenal existence. You take the cocooner to the self-existing playground, which includes both setting-sun and Great Eastern Sun displays of all kinds. The playground is self-existing because it's not something we manufacture. It's a natural situation.

It's a little bit like going to Disneyland. You might say that Disneyland has the ultimate setting-sun possibilities, but it is also very well intentioned. At Disneyland there is a lot of goodness, gentleness, and humor that is almost comparable to the level of the Great Eastern Sun, and which doesn't seem to be purely based on financial gain. The self-existing playground is like that. It is a display of phenomena that can be seen as both a setting-sun and a Great Eastern Sun situation. When there is mutual humor, that kind of connection comes through.

The next stage is quite serious. It's a major step. The cocooner steps out of the baby stroller and begins to walk, taking a few little steps. The first experience of this is shocking. There is no gentle transition. And then, to promote the primordial confidence of the would-be warrior, suddenly the cocooner is presented with a weapon.

That's quite a dangerous thing to do. We don't do this with human infants. You don't give babies a knife and fork, because they might do something funny with those implements. They might stab themselves. But here, the cocooners are not actual infants. They may be eighty years old or twenty-five years old or sixteen. However, we should remember that we're not talking about bringing up babies here. We are talking in terms of how to actually inspire grown-up people to step out of their cocoons. So in this case, we take the cocooners to the archery range of the warriors, which possesses primordial confidence. We let the cocooners shoot arrows, play with the bow, and acknowledge the target.

Stepping out of the baby stroller is the first real breakthrough. When you take them to the archery range, the would-be warriors begin to click in and connect, because they do possess primordial confidence within themselves. They possess basic goodness, basic humanness, basic warriorness. Therefore, they may wake into their primordial nature.

To help them awaken, the cocooners are finally introduced to their neighbors, fellow warriors, as well as to their aunts and uncles and the elder statesmen, the elder warriors of the Shambhala world. If you tried to introduce them to such people too soon, they might say "Waaah! I don't want anything to do with this." So first we let them play with the instruments of warriorship, with bows and arrows, which are half toy, half weapon. Then, after they go to the archery range, they begin to connect with the elder statesmen, who represent the best of human society or the society of warriors, which possesses beauty and dignity.

When the cocooners connect to this, then they can go out without any stroller at all. They can walk by themselves, and they might begin to dress up in elegant suits and dresses, or suits of armor, whatever they have. The cocooners have finally been transformed into fully human beings.

Then, the fearful mind can actually be converted into the mind of the warrior. The cocooner has ceased to be a cocooner. He or she has long since forgotten the cocoon, although he still might want to jump back into his stroller. But the real connection to the warrior's world has been made. It is not really so much that the cocooner's mind is changing into the warrior's mind, but he is realizing his innate nature, which is basically good.

Since the cocooner has now become a warrior, she begins to realize eternal youthful confidence. This confidence is connected with experiencing the first glimpse of magic in her state of being. Her mind begins to relax. She begins to develop a natural state of goodness that has no beginning or end. At that point, when wakefulness begins to take place, the cocooner is finally transformed into a real warrior who will experience the Great Eastern Sun.

8

Nonviolence

IN THE LAST CHAPTER, we looked at the would-be warrior as an infant in the cocoon. There is another way we could describe the education of the warrior, which is by looking at the development of ego and how the warrior works with fear and other problems that arise from a mistaken belief in the self as a solid entity.

From this point of view, the ego feels rather lonely and, at the same time, keeps busy trying to defend itself. It finds that it consists of a collection of desires, expectations, ideas, conclusions, memories, and many other things. This collection is too complex for the ego to grasp; therefore, it conveniently constructs "I am" or "I am the ego" and tends to put this label on itself, as if it were a real individual entity. Having found a name for itself, the ego has to constantly work to secure itself, because fundamentally it knows that it is not real and sound. So ego keeps busy trying to build a wall around itself, to shut itself away from the "other." Then, of course, having created this barrier, immediately the ego also wants to communicate with the other, which it now perceives as "outside" or not part of itself.

If anyone gets too near the wall that ego has built, it feels insecure. It thinks that it is being attacked and then thinks that the only way to defend itself is to ward off the threat by showing an aggressive attitude. However, when one experiences a threat that seems to come from outside—whether it is illness, some undesirable experience in the world, or literal opponents— the only way to develop a balanced state of being is not to try to get rid of those things, but to understand them and make use of them. Thus, the development of egolessness—the opposite of ego's game—leads one to the concept of ahimsa, or nonviolence. Ahimsa is a nonviolent way of dealing with a situation. It is the warrior's way.

To develop the nonviolent approach, first of all you have to see that your problems are not really trying to destroy you. Usually, we immediately try to get rid of our problems. We think that there are forces operating against us that we have to overpower. The important thing is to learn to be friendly toward our problems, by developing what is called maitri in Sanskrit or loving-kindness in English translation. All of these problems and difficulties are fundamentally generated from the concept of duality or separateness. On the one hand, you are very aware of others and also very aware of yourself, and you want to do something to work with and make use of others. But you are unable to do this because there is such a big gap between others and yourself. So a sense of threat and separation develops. That is the root of the problem.

At a certain point, you develop a genuine aspiration to get rid of the wall—the separation between you and others. However, you should not think in terms of having to fight with and defeat these problems. Furthermore, you should not develop the idea of being on a battlefield, because this just solidifies the problems. In relationship to this situation, the martial arts are quite interesting, because of their way of dealing with problems and exercising the real art of war.

To work with this dichotomy of self and others, first it is necessary to consider the facts and patterns of life, that is, your behavior, your approach to communication, and your way of life overall. There are certain aspects of your life that are not balanced, but those very things can be developed into a balanced state of being, which is the main thing that we need to achieve. Three things make for imbalance: ignorance, hatred, and desire. Now, the fact is, they are not bad. Good and bad have nothing to do with this. Rather, we are dealing only with imbalance and balance. We are not purely discussing the spiritual aspect of our lives or the mundane aspect, but the whole of life. In the unbalanced way of behaving, one does not deal properly with a situation. One's action is not appropriate. One action overlaps another, and the action is not fully completed. This boils down to not being fully aware in the situation and not feeling present. The present moment of action is not properly accomplished, for when a person is halfway through dealing with the present action, he is already drifting on to the next action. This produces a kind of indigestion in the mind, for there is something always left incomplete, like leaving a fruit half eaten.

If you are picking fruit from a tree, you may see a particular piece of fruit that looks delicious, ready to eat. You really want to eat that one. But as you are biting into it, you see another fruit on the tree, one that looks even better. So you immediately leap up and grab that piece of fruit as well. In that way, you keep stuffing yourself with one fruit after another. You end up eating fruit that is not properly ripened, which finally produces indigestion.

Therefore, the idea of balance is very down-to-earth and simple. There are certain patterns of behavior that are not balanced, and that are caused by either ignorance, hatred, passion, or a combination of these factors.

Ignorance in this case means that someone is not able to accomplish his or her present work thoroughly. Ignorance ignores what is, because your mind is occupied by either experiences from the past or expectations of the future. Therefore, you are never able to be *now*. Ignorance means ignoring the present.

Another problem is aggression. If you are aggressive, in terms of your emotions or your sentiments, you are not developing your strength at all, but you are just trying to defend yourself in a rather feeble and clumsy way. In the state of aggression, you are constantly trying to fight with someone else. Your mind is so occupied with your opponent that you are continuously defensive, trying to defend yourself in the fear that something will happen to you. Therefore, you are not able to see a positive alternative, one that would allow you to actually deal effectively with problems. Instead, your mind is clouded, and you do not have the clarity of mind to deal with situations. The ability to respond and act appropriately in situations has nothing to do with cranking up aggression. On the other hand, it is not particularly based on the pacifist idea of not fighting at all. We have to try to find a middle ground, where one engages the energy fully but without any aggression.

The real way of the warrior is not to become aggressive and not to act against or be hostile to other people. Normally, when we hear that there is some challenge to overcome, we tend to think of an aggressive action or response, which is wrong. We have to learn that aggression is quite different from using or channeling our energy properly.

According to some traditional Chinese Buddhist sources, monks in some monasteries practiced judo, karate, and other martial arts—but not in order to challenge, kill, or destroy other people. Rather, they used these martial arts to learn to control their minds and to develop a balanced way of dealing with situations without involving oneself in hatred and the panic of ego. When one practices the martial arts, one appears to be engaged in aggressive activities. Nevertheless, one is not fundamentally being aggressive, from the point of view of generating or acting out of hatred. The true practice of the martial arts is a question of developing a state in which one is fully confident, fully knowing what one is and what one is trying to do.

What is necessary is to learn to understand the other side of any situation, to make friends with the opponent or the problem in order to see the opponent clearly and to understand what move he is going to make next. In Tibet, this idea is put into practice in the study of logic. When I was studying in Tibet, we learned a very elaborate system of logic, where you don't just argue a point any way you want to, but you have to use particular logical rules and terms. When your opponent in a debate makes an argument, you are allowed to answer with only one of four possible responses: "Why?" "Not quite so," "Wrong," or "No." These are the only four answers you can give. The other person can make their argument and attack you in many different ways, but you can only use these four phrases to refute them. In order to choose the right phrase, you must know exactly what your opponent is going to say in the next ten minutes. You don't just know; you *feel* it, because you are one with the situation. Theoretically at least, you don't have any combative feelings toward your opponent. Therefore, there is no aggression to produce a blinding effect on you or to make you ignorant of what is going on. You see the situation very clearly, and you're able to deal with it more effectively.

In general, if you want to develop a really effective way of challenging something, you have to develop a lot of maitri, or loving-kindness, toward your opponents. The term *loving-kindness* or even *compassion* is generally rather sentimental and rather weak in the English language. It has certain connotations connected with the popular concept of charity and being kind to your neighbors. The concept of maitri is different from that. In part, of course, it does involve a sentimental approach, since there is always room for emotions. However, maitri is not just being kind and nice. It is the understanding that one has to become one with the situation. That does not particularly mean that one becomes entirely without personality and has to accept whatever the other person suggests. Rather, you have to overcome the barrier that you have formed between yourself and others. If you remove this barrier and open yourself, then automatically real understanding and clarity will develop in your mind. The whole point is that, in order to successfully challenge someone, first of all you must develop loving-kindness and a feeling of longing for openness, so that there is no desire to challenge anyone at all. If one has a desire to conquer or win a challenge against another, then in the process of challenging him or her, the mind is filled with this desire and one is not really able to challenge the other properly. Going beyond challenge is learning the art of war.

Real warriors do not think in terms of challenge, nor are their minds occupied with the battlefield or with past or future consequences. The warrior is completely one with bravery, one with that particular moment. He or she is fully concentrated in the moment, because he knows the art of war. You are entirely skilled in your tactics: you do not refer to past events or develop your strength through thinking about future consequences and victory. You are fully aware at that moment, which automatically brings success in the challenge.

From this point of view, it is very important that the warrior really be able to become one with the situation and develop maitri. Then the whole force of opposition becomes one with you. The opposing force needs another strength coming, advancing, toward him. As the opponent is approaching you, the closer he gets, he expects more and more to encounter another strength coming toward him. When that strength is not there at all, he just collapses. He misses the target, collapses, and his whole force becomes self-defeating. It is like someone trying to fight his hallucinations: as he tries to strike them harder, he himself falls on the ground. That is the whole point: when you do not produce another force of hatred, the opposing force collapses. This is also connected with how to deal with one's thoughts in the practice of meditation. If you do not try to repress your thoughts, but you just accept them and don't get involved with them, then the whole structure of thoughts becomes one with you and is no longer disturbing.

The practice of yoga, which has been taught through the Indian tradition, also has some connections with the nonviolent art of war. In yoga everything is based on the concept of uncovering strength within oneself. This is different from the ordinary idea of developing strength. Generally, we tend to think of strength as developing the power to overcome or control someone else. We think of strength as a force that we are lacking, which can be found and developed in order to challenge and defeat someone.

In the proper practice of yoga, as well as within the martial arts, one's strength or power comes from the development of a balanced state of mind altogether. That is to say, one is going back, or returning, to the origin of the strength that exists within oneself. If one had to develop new strength through gymnastics or physical practices alone, such strength created out of gymnastic practice, as it were, would have no mental strength to reinforce it, and it would tend to collapse. But the kind of strength we are talking about here is known as strength in its own right, the strength of fearlessness (*jigme* in Tibetan). To be without fear is to have great strength. The realization of fearlessness is the genuine martial art.

Part Two

THE PATH OF FEARLESSNESS

A warrior should be capable of artfully conducting his or her life in every action, from drinking tea to running a country. Learning how to handle fear, and how to utilize both our own and other people's fear, is what allows us to brew the beer of fearlessness. You can put all of those situations of fear and doubt into a gigantic vat and ferment them.

The path of fearlessness is connected with what we do right now, today, rather than with anything theoretical or waiting for a cue from somewhere else. The basic vision of warriorship is that there is goodness in everyone. We are all good in ourselves. So we have our own warrior society within our own body. We have everything we need to make the journey already.

9

Overcoming Doubt

WHEN WE BRING TOGETHER the ancient spiritual traditions of East and West, we find a meeting point where
the warrior tradition can be experienced and realized. The concept of being a warrior is applicable to the most basic situations
in our lives—to the fundamental situation that exists before
the notion of good or bad ever occurs. The term *warrior* relates
to the basic situation of being a human being. The heart of the
warrior is this basic aliveness or basic goodness. Such fearless
goodness is free from doubt and overcomes any perverted attitudes toward reality.

Doubt is the first obstacle to fearlessness that has to be overcome. We're not talking here about suppressing your doubts
about a particular thing that is taking place. Nor are we talking
about having doubts about joining an organization, or something like that. We are referring here to overcoming a much
more basic doubt, which is fundamentally doubting yourself
and feeling that you have shortcomings as a human being. You
don't feel that your mind and body are synchronized or working together properly. You feel that you are constantly being
shortchanged somewhere in your life.

When you were growing up, at a very early stage—perhaps
around two years old—you must have heard your father or
mother saying no to you. They would say, "No, don't get into

that," or "No, don't explore that too much," or "No, be quiet. Be still." When you heard the word *no*, you may have responded by trying to fulfill that *no*, by being good. Or you may have reacted negatively, by defying your parents and their *no*, by exploring further and being "bad." That mixture of the temptation to be naughty and the desire to be disciplined occurs very early in life. When our parents say no to us, it makes us feel strange about ourselves, which becomes an expression of fear.

On the other hand, there is another kind of *no*, which is very positive. We have never heard that basic *no* properly: a *no* free from fear and free from doubt. Instead, even if we think that we're doing our best in life, we still feel that we haven't fully lived up to what we should be. We feel that we're not quite doing things right. We feel that our parents or others don't approve of us. There is that fundamental doubt, or fundamental fear, as to whether or not we can actually accomplish something.

Doubt arises in relating with authority, discipline, and scheduling throughout our life. When we don't acknowledge our doubt, it manifests as resistance and resentment. There is often some resentment or a reaction against the sitting practice of meditation as well. The moment that a gong is struck to signal the beginning of meditation practice, we feel resistance. But in that situation, we find that it's too late. We're already sitting there on the cushion, so we usually continue to practice.

However, resistance in everyday life provides us with many ways to manipulate situations. When we are presented with a challenge, we often try to turn away rather than having to face it. We come up with all kinds of excuses to avoid the demands that we feel are being put on us.

The basic *no*, on the other hand, is accepting discipline in our life without preconceptions. Normally, when we say the word "discipline," it comes with a lot of mixed feelings. It's like saying "oatmeal." Some people like hot cereal and some people hate it. Nevertheless, oatmeal remains oatmeal. It is a very straightforward thing. We have similar feelings about discipline and the meaning of *no*. Sometimes, it's a bad *no*: it is providing oppressive boundaries that we don't want to accept. Or it could be a good *no*, which encourages us to do something healthy. But when we just hear that one word, *no*, the message is mixed.

Fearlessness is extending ourselves beyond that limited view. The *Heart Sutra*, an essential teaching given by the Buddha, talks about going beyond. "Gone beyond," *gate* in Sanskrit, is the basic *no*. The sutra says there is no eye, no ear, no sound, no smell—none of those things. When you experience egolessness, the solidity of your life and your perceptions falls apart. That could be very desolate or it could be very inspiring, in terms of shunyata, the Buddhist understanding of emptiness. Very simply, it is basic *no*. It is a real expression of fearlessness. In the Buddhist view, egolessness is preexisting, beyond our preconceptions. In the state of egolessness everything is simple and very clear. When we try to supplement the brightness of egolessness by putting a lot of other things onto it, those things obscure its brilliance, becoming blockages and veils.

In the warrior tradition, sacred outlook is the brilliant environment created by basic goodness. When we refuse to have any contact with that state of being, when we turn away from basic goodness, then wrong beliefs arise. We come up with all sorts of logics, again and again, so that we don't have to face the realities of the world.

We run up against our hesitation to get fully into things all the time, even in seemingly insignificant situations. If we don't want to wash the dishes right after we've eaten, we may tell ourselves that we need to let them soak. In fact we're often hoping that one of our housemates will clean up after us. On another level, philosophically speaking, we may feel completely tuned in to the warrior's world. From that point of view, we think that we can quite safely say, "Once a warrior, always a warrior." That sounds good, but in terms of the actual *practice* of warriorship, it's questionable. "Once a warrior" may not always be a warrior if we disregard the beauty of the phenomenal world. We prefer to wear sunglasses rather than face the brilliance of the sunshine. (Of course, I'm not speaking literally here, since you might very well need to protect yourself from the damaging rays of the sun.) We put on a hat and gloves to shield ourselves, fearing that we might get burned. The colorfulness of relationships, household chores, business enterprises, and our general livelihood are too irritating. We are constantly looking for padding so that we don't run into the sharp edges of the world. That is the essence of wrong belief. It is an obstacle to seeing the wisdom of the Great Eastern Sun, which is seeing a greater vision beyond our own small world.

The ground of fearlessness, which is the basis for overcoming doubt and wrong belief, is the development of renunciation. Renunciation here means overcoming that very hard and tough aggressive mentality which wards off any gentleness that might come into our hearts. Fear does not allow fundamental tenderness to enter into us. When tenderness tinged by sadness touches our heart, we know that we are in contact with reality. We feel it. That contact is genuine, fresh, and quite raw. That sensitivity is the basic experience of warriorship, and it is the key to developing fearless renunciation.

Sometimes people find that being tender and raw is threatening and seemingly exhausting. Openness seems demanding and energy-consuming, so they prefer to cover up their tender heart. Vulnerability can sometimes make you nervous. It is uncomfortable to feel so real, so you want to numb yourself. You look for some kind of anesthetic, anything that will provide you with entertainment. Then you can forget the discomfort of reality. People don't want to live with their basic rawness for even fifteen minutes. When people say they are bored, often they mean that they don't want to experience the sense of emptiness, which is also an expression of openness and vulnerability. So they pick up the newspaper or read anything else that's lying around the room—even reading what it says on a cereal box to keep themselves entertained. The search for entertainment to babysit your boredom soon becomes legitimized as laziness. Such laziness actually involves a lot of exertion. You have to constantly crank things up to occupy yourself with, overcoming your boredom by indulging in laziness.

For the warrior, fearlessness is the opposite of that approach. Fearlessness is a question of learning how to be. Be there all along: that is the message. That is quite challenging in what we call the setting-sun world, the world of neurotic comfort where we use everything to fill up the space. We even use our emotions to entertain ourselves. You might be genuinely angry about something for a fraction of a second, but then you draw out your anger so that it lasts for twenty-five minutes. Then you crank up something else to be angry at for the next twenty minutes. Sometimes, if you arouse a really good attack of anger, it can last for days and days. That is another way we entertain ourselves in the setting-sun world.

The remedy to that approach is renunciation. In the Buddhist teachings, renunciation is associated with being nauseated and pained by samsara, the confused world. For the warrior, renunciation is slightly different. It is giving away, or not indulging in, pleasure for entertainment's sake. We are going to kick out any preoccupations provided by the miscellaneous babysitters in the phenomenal world.

Finally, renunciation is the willingness to work with real situations of aggression in the world. If someone interrupts your world with an attack of aggression, you have to respond to it. There is no other way. Renunciation is being willing to face that intense kind of situation rather than cover it up. Everyone is afraid to talk about this. It may be shocking to mention it. Nonetheless, we have to learn to relate to those aspects of the world. We have never developed any response to attack—whether it is a verbal attack or actual physical aggression. People are very shy of this topic, although we have the answers to these challenges in our warrior disciplines: our exertion and our manifestation, or general state of being.

In the warrior tradition, fearlessness is connected with attaching your basic existence to greater vision, the Great Eastern Sun. In order to experience such vast and demanding vision, you need a real connection to basic goodness. The key to that is overcoming doubt and wrong belief. Doubt is your own internal problem, which you have to work with. But then beyond that there may be an enemy, a challenge, that is outside of you. We can't just pretend that those threats never exist. You might say that your laziness is some kind of enemy, but laziness is not actually an enemy. It would be better to call it an obstacle.

How are we going to respond to real opposition when it arises in the world? As a warrior, how are you going to relate with that? You don't need party-line logic or a package-deal response. They don't really help. In my experience of how students usually relate with conflict, I find that they tend to freeze up when someone is very critical of them. They become noncommunicative, which doesn't help the situation. As warriors, we shouldn't be uptight and uncommunicative. We find it easy to manifest basic goodness when somebody agrees with us. Even if they're half-agreeing with you, you can talk to them and have a great time. But if someone is edgy and negative, then you freeze, become defensive, and begin to attack them back. That's the wrong end of the stick. You don't kill an enemy before they become the enemy. You only slash the enemy when they become a hundred percent good enemy and present a real hundred percent challenge. If you're attracted to someone who is interested in making love with you, you make love with them. But you don't rape them. This is the same idea.

When a warrior has to kill his enemy, he has a very soft heart. He looks his enemy right in the face. The grip on your sword is quite strong and tough, and then with a tender heart, you cut your enemy into two pieces. At that point, slashing your enemy is equivalent to making love to them. That very strong, powerful stroke is also sympathetic. That fearless stroke is frightening, don't you think? We don't want to face that possibility.

On the other hand, if we are in touch with basic goodness, we are always relating to the world directly, choicelessly, whether the energy of the situation demands a destructive or a constructive response. The idea of renunciation is to relate with whatever arises with a sense of sadness and tenderness. We reject the aggressive, hard-core street-fighter mentality. The neurotic upheavals created by overcoming conflicting emotions, or the kleshas, arise from ignorance, or avidya. This is fundamental ignorance that underlies all ego-oriented activity. Ignorance is very harsh and willing to stick with its own version of things. Therefore, it feels very righteous. Overcoming that is the essence of renunciation: we have no hard edges.

Warriorship is so tender, without skin, without tissue, naked and raw. It is soft and gentle. You have renounced putting on a new suit of armor. You have renounced growing a thick, hard skin. You are willing to expose naked flesh, bone, and marrow to the world.

This whole discussion is not just metaphoric. We are talking about what you do if you actually have to slash the enemy, if you are in combat or having a sword fight with someone, as you see in Japanese samurai movies. We shouldn't be too cowardly. A sword fight is real, as real as making love to another human being. We are talking about direct experience, and we're not psychologizing anything here. Before you slash the enemy, look into his or her eyes and feel that tenderness. Then you slash. When you slash your enemy, your compassionate heart becomes twice as big. It puffs up; it becomes a big heart; therefore you can slash the enemy. If you are small-hearted, you cannot do this properly.

Of course, many times conquering the enemy might not involve cutting them in two. You might just turn them upside down! But you have to be willing to face the possibilities.

When the warrior has thoroughly experienced his or her own basic rawness, there is no room to manipulate the situation. You just go forward and present the truth quite fearlessly. You can be what you are, in a very straightforward and basic way. So tenderness brings simplicity and naturalness, almost at the level of simplemindedness.

We don't want to become tricky warriors, with all kinds of tricks up our sleeves and ways to cut people's logic down when we don't agree with them. Then there is no cultivation of either ourselves or others. When that occurs, we destroy any possibilities of enlightened society. In fact, there will be no society; just a few people hanging out. Instead, the fearless warriors of Shambhala are very ordinary, simpleminded warriors. That is the starting point for developing true bravery.

10

The Tools of Bravery

THE PATH OF FEARLESSNESS begins with the discovery of fear. We find ourselves fearful, frightened, even petrified by circumstances. This ubiquitous nervousness provides us with a stepping-stone so that we can step over our fear. We have to make a definite move to cross over the boundary from cowardice to bravery. If we do so properly, the other side of our cowardice contains bravery.

We may not discover bravery right away. Instead, beyond our nervousness, we find a shaky tenderness. We are still quivering, but we are shaking with tenderness rather than bewilderment. That shaky vulnerability contains an element of sadness, but not in the sense of feeling bad about oneself or feeling deprived. Rather, we feel a natural sense of fullness that is tender and sad.

It's like the feeling you have when you are about to shed a tear. You feel somewhat wealthy because your eyes are full of tears. When you blink, tears begin to roll down your cheeks. There is also an element of loneliness, but again it is not based on deprivation, inadequacy, or rejection. Instead you feel that you alone can understand the truth of your own loneliness, which is quite dignified and self-contained. You have a full heart, you feel lonely, but you don't feel particularly bad about it. It is like an island in the middle of a lake. The island is self-contained; therefore it looks lonely in the middle of the water. Ferryboats occasionally carry commuters back and forth from the shore to the island, but that doesn't particularly help. In fact, it expresses the loneliness or the aloneness of the island even more.

Discovering these facets of fearlessness is preparation for the further journey on the warrior's path. If the warrior does not feel alone and sad, then he or she can be corrupted very easily. In fact, such a person may not be a warrior *at all*. To be a good warrior, one has to feel sad and lonely, but rich and resourceful at the same time. This makes the warrior sensitive to every aspect of phenomena: to sights, smells, sounds, and feelings. In that sense, the warrior is also an artist, appreciating whatever goes on in the world. Everything is extremely vivid. The rustling of your armor or the sound of raindrops falling on your coat is very loud. The fluttering of occasional butterflies around you is almost an insult, because you are so sensitive.

Such a sensitive warrior can then go further on the path of fearlessness. There are three tools or practical guides that the warrior uses on this journey. The first is the development of discipline, or *shila* in Sanskrit, which is represented by the analogy of the sun. Sunshine is all-pervasive. When the sun shines on the land, it doesn't neglect any area. It does a thorough job. Similarly, as a warrior, you never neglect your discipline. We're not talking about military rigidity here. Rather, in all your mannerisms, every aspect of behavior, you maintain your openness to the environment. You constantly extend yourself to things around you.

There is a complete absence of laziness. Even if what you are seeing, hearing, or perceiving becomes very difficult and demanding, the warrior never gives up. You go along with the situation. You don't withdraw. This allows you to develop your loyalty and connection to others, free from fear. You can relate with other sentient beings who are trapped in the confused world, perpetuating their pain. In fact, you realize that it is your duty. You feel warmth, compassion, and even passion toward others. First you develop your own good conduct, and then you can extend yourself fearlessly to others. That is the concept of the sun.

The second guide on the warrior's path is represented by the analogy of an echo, which is connected with meditative awareness, or *samadhi*. When you try to take time off from being a warrior, when you want to let go of your discipline or indulge mindlessly in some activity, your action produces an echo. It's like a sound echoing in a canyon, bouncing back on itself, producing more echoes that bounce off one another. Those echoes or reflections happen all the time, and if we pay attention to them, they provide constant reminders to be awake. At first, the reminder might be fairly timid, but then the second, third, and fourth time you hear it, it's a much louder echo. These echoes remind you to be on the spot, on the dot. However, you can't just wait for an echo to wake you up. You have to put your awareness out into the situation. You have to put effort into being aware.

Becoming a warrior means that you are building a world that does not give you the degraded, setting-sun concept of rest, which is purely indulging in your confusion. Sometimes you are tempted to return to that cowardly world. You just want to flop and forget the echo of your awareness. It seems like a tremendous relief not to have to work so hard. But then you discover that this world without even an echo is too deadly. You find it refreshing to get back to the warrior's world, because it is so much more alive.

The warrior's third tool is actually a weapon. It is represented by the analogy of a bow and arrow, which is connected with developing wisdom, or prajna, and skillful means, or *upaya*. Prajna is the wisdom of discriminating awareness, which is experiencing the sharpness of sense perceptions and developing psychological accuracy. This is the same quality of natural intelligence we discussed earlier as the sun in your head. Here you are wielding that intelligence as a weapon of awareness. You can't develop this kind of sharpness unless some experience of egolessness has manifested in your mind. Otherwise, your mind will be preoccupied, full of its own ego. But when you have made a connection with basic goodness, you can relate with both the actual sharpness of the arrow and with the skillful means provided by the bow. The bow allows you to harness or execute the sharpness of your perceptions.

The development of this discriminating-awareness wisdom also allows you to accurately detect the enemy. A real enemy is someone who propagates and promotes ultimate selfishness, or ego. Such enemies promote basic badness rather than basic goodness. They try to bring others into their realm, tempting them with anything from a cookie up to a million dollars.

In the Shambhala warrior tradition, we say that you should only have to kill an enemy once every thousand years. We mean here the real enemy, the basic *rudra* principle, which is the personification of egohood, or ego run wild. You can work with other enemies by subjugating or pacifying them, talking to them, buying them out, or seducing them. However, according to this tradition, once in a thousand years a real assassination of the ultimate enemy may be necessary. We're talking about an extremely rare situation in which someone can't be reached by any other means. Your action has to be completely free from aggression, and it cannot be motivated by anger, greed, or a desire for retribution or vengeance. The motivation has to be pure compassion. You might use a sword or an arrow, whatever means you need to overpower them, so that their ego is completely popped. Such an assassination has to be very direct and personal. It's not like dropping bombs on people. If we pop the enemy, and only then, they might be able to connect with some basic goodness within themselves and realize that they made a gigantic mistake. You always look for other alternatives to cure the situation, but sometimes there are none. It's like having rotten teeth in your mouth. Eventually you have to have all your teeth removed, replacing them with false teeth. After that, you might be able to appreciate the teeth that you lost.

Overall, these three principles—the sun, the echo, and the bow and arrow—are all connected with the natural process, or path, of working with our basic intelligence. Beyond that, they describe the fundamental decorum and decency of the warrior's existence. A warrior should be capable of artfully conducting his or her life in every action, from drinking tea to running a country. Learning how to handle fear, and how to utilize both our own and other people's fear, is what allows us to brew the beer of fearlessness. You can put all of those situations of fear and doubt into a gigantic vat and ferment them.

The path of fearlessness is connected with what we do right now, today, rather than with anything theoretical or waiting for a cue from somewhere else. The basic vision of warriorship is that there is goodness in everyone. We are all good in ourselves. So we have our own warrior society within our own body. We have everything we need to make the journey already.

11

Unconditional Fearlessness

FEARLESSNESS has a starting point, it includes discipline, it makes a journey, and it reaches a conclusion. It is like the Great Eastern Sun: the sun rises, it radiates light, and this benefits people by dispelling the darkness and allowing the fruit to ripen and the flowers to blossom.

The fruition of fearlessness is connected with three analogies. The first is that fearlessness is like a reservoir of trust. This trust arises from the experience of basic goodness, which we have already discussed. When we feel basically good, rather than degraded or condemned, then we become very inquisitive, looking into every situation and examining it. We don't want to fool ourselves by relying on belief alone. Rather, we want to make a personal connection with reality.

The reservoir of trust is a very simple, straightforward idea. If we accept a challenge and take certain steps to accomplish something, the process will yield results—either success or failure. When you sow a seed or plant a tree, either the seed will germinate, the tree will grow, or it will die. Similarly, for the inquisitive warrior, trust means that we know that our actions will bring a definite response from reality. We know that we will get a message. Failure generally is telling us that our action has been undisciplined and inaccurate in some way. Therefore, it fails. When our action is fully disciplined, it usually is fulfilled;

we have success. But those responses are not regarded as either punishment or congratulations.

Trust, then, is being willing to take a chance, knowing that what goes up must come down, as they say. When a warrior has that kind of trust in the reflections of the phenomenal world, then she can trust her individual discovery of goodness. Communication produces results: either success or failure. That is how the fearless warrior relates with the universe, not by remaining alone and insecure, hiding away, but by constantly being exposed to the phenomenal world and constantly being willing to take that chance.

The reservoir of trust is a bank of richness from which the warrior can always draw conclusions. We begin to feel that we are dealing with a rich world, one that never runs out of messages. The only problem arises if we try to manipulate the situation in our favor. You are not supposed to fish in the reservoir or swim in it. The reservoir has to remain unconditional, unpolluted. So you don't put your one-sided bias, or conditionality, into it. Then the reservoir might dry up.

Normally, trust means that we think that our world is trustworthy. We think that it's going to produce a good result, success. But in this case, we're talking about having a continual relationship with the phenomenal world that is not based on either a good or a bad result. We unconditionally trust the phenomenal world to always give us a message, either success or failure. The fruition of our action will always provide us with information. Such trust in the reservoir keeps us from being too arrogant or too timid. If you're too arrogant, you'll find yourself bumping into the ceiling. If you're too timid, you'll be pushed up by the floor. Roughly speaking, that's the concept of the reservoir.

The ancient Chinese *Book of Changes,* or *I Ching,* often talks about success being failure and failure being success. Success sows the seeds of future failure, and failure may bring a later success. So it's always a dynamic process. For warriors, fearlessness doesn't mean that we cheer up by saying "Look! I'm on the side of the right. I'm a success." Nor do we feel that we're being punished when we fail. In any case, success and failure are saying the same thing.

That brings us to the next analogy, which is music. Music is connected with the idea of continuously being joyful. The feedback or the result that comes from the warrior's practice is never a dead end. It presents another path. We always can go on, go beyond. So while the result of action is fruition, beyond that, the result is the seed for the next journey. Our journey continues, cycling between success and failure, path and fruition, just as the four seasons alternate. There is always further creativity, so there is always joy on the journey, joy in the result.

Why are you so joyful? You are guided on the path by the disciplines of the sun, the echo, and the bow and arrow. You have witnessed your basic goodness, taking joy in having nothing to hang on to. You have realized the fundamental *no*. You are free from doubt and you have experienced a sense of renunciation. So whether the situation brings success or failure, it brings an unconditional good understanding. Therefore, your mind and body are constantly synchronized; there is no deficit of any kind in the body or the mind. Your experience becomes like music, which has rhythm and a melody that is constantly expanding and being re-created. So the sense of celebration is constant, built-in, in spite of the ups and downs of one's personal life. That is continuously being joyful.

Having developed trust and appreciation, you can finally conquer fear, which is connected with the analogy of a saddle. In the Buddhist teachings we talk about developing such a good sense of mental balance that, if you become mindless, your awareness automatically brings you back, just as in the process of skidding on the ice and losing your balance, your body automatically rebalances itself to keep from falling. In the saddle, as long as you have good posture and a good seat, you can overcome any startling or unexpected moves your horse makes. So the idea of the saddle is taking a good seat in your life.

An overreaction or an exaggerated reaction to situations shouldn't happen at this level. You have trust, you are constantly being joyful, and therefore you can't be startled either. This doesn't mean that your life is monotone, but rather you feel established in this world. You belong here. You are one of the warriors in this world, so even if little unexpected things happen, good or bad, right or wrong, you don't exaggerate them. You come back to your seat in the saddle and maintain your posture in the situation.

The warrior is never amazed by anything. If someone comes up to you and says, "I'm going to kill you right now," you are not amazed. If someone says they are going to give you a million dollars, you think, "So what?" Assuming your seat in the saddle at this level is achieving inscrutability, in the positive sense.

It is also taking your seat on the earth. Once you have a good seat on the earth, you don't need witnesses to validate you. Someone once asked the Buddha, "How do we know that you are enlightened?" He touched the earth in the gesture known as the earth-touching mudra and said, "Earth is my witness." That is the same concept as holding your seat in the saddle. Someone might ask, "How do we know you won't overreact to this situation?" You can say, "Just watch my posture in the saddle."

Fearlessness in the warrior tradition is not training yourself in ultimate paranoia. It is based on training in ultimate solidity—which is basic goodness. You have to learn how to be regal. Trust is like becoming a good citizen, celebrating the journey is like becoming a good minister in the government, but holding your seat in the saddle is finally assuming command. It is how to be a king or queen.

At the same time, conquering fear is not based on blocking your sensitivity. Otherwise, you become a deaf and dumb monarch, a jellyfish king. Sitting on the horse requires balance, and as you acquire that balance in the saddle, you have more awareness of the horse. So, when you sit in the saddle on your fickle horse, you feel completely exposed and gentle. If you feel aggressive, you don't have a good seat. In fact, you are probably not even riding the horse. You don't put your saddle on a fence railing; you have to saddle a real horse. In this case, riding the horse is riding somebody else's mind. It requires complete connection, or working with the other person. In the Buddhist tradition, this is called compassion. You are completely exposed in this situation. Otherwise, it's like a medieval knight encased in his armor. It's so heavy that he has to be cranked up onto the horse. Then he rides off to battle and usually falls off. There's something wrong with that technology.

Often, when someone tells us not to be afraid, we think they're saying not to worry, that everything is going to be all right. Unconditional fearlessness, however, is simply based on being awake. Once you have command of the situation, fearlessness is unconditional because you are neither on the side of success nor on the side of failure. Success *and* failure are your journey.

Nevertheless, sometimes you become so petrified on your journey that your teeth, your eyes, your hands, and your legs are all vibrating. You are hardly sitting in your seat; you are practically levitating with fear. But even that is regarded as an expression of fearlessness if you have a fundamental connection with the earth of basic goodness—which is unconditional goodness at this point.

12

Joining Heaven and Earth

O UR NEXT TOPIC is joining heaven and earth together, which is to some extent the natural outgrowth of the disciplines we discussed in the last three chapters. At the same time, joining heaven and earth has it own logic that can be applied to our journey as a whole. In this case, heaven is our state of mind, and earth is our physical body and surroundings. When mind and body are joined together properly, there is a sense of joining heaven and earth. This comes from the sitting practice of meditation, to begin with. We have to sit and slow down. The discipline of meditation is both training the mind and training the body. In the discipline of meditation, we have both a constant posture of uprightness, which is the quality of body, and a means of relating with the greater depth of space, or experiencing great openness, which is working with our mind.

When you practice, your posture is very important. Ordinarily what we call a relaxed posture is actually rather hunched over. In the practice of meditation, your posture doesn't have to be stiff, but it needs to be upright. Your spine should feel straight. On the other hand, you don't want to be so rigid that it's lifeless, like a wax figure. Your shoulders should feel natural. Check your body before you get into your practice. When you sit down to practice, first check your spine, from your waist up to your shoulders. Then check your shoulders themselves, and finally check your neck. Your seat should be solid, and your posture should feel uplifted and definite, but still relaxed.

The traditional analogy is that your posture should be like a king or queen sitting on a throne. In this case, of course, we are speaking of an enlightened monarch, a Shambhala monarch, rather than any old monarch sitting on the throne, with his or her head made heavy by the crown. This everyday monarch feels uncomfortable and hopes that the day's events will end as soon as possible. By contrast, the Shambhala monarch is quite happy to be there.

When mind and body are synchronized in your life and practice, there is very little chance for neurosis of any kind to arise. The basis of neurosis, or even physical discomfort and pain, is mind and body not joining together. Sometimes the mind is miles away and the body is here. Or the body is miles away and the mind is there. The main point of practice is learning to be a proper human being, which is known as being a warrior. When mind and body are joined together, then you are joining heaven and earth, and you can be a genuine warrior. This quality of harmony will bring fearlessness. However, this fearlessness will also be punctuated by occasional fear, uncertainty, and confusion.

Fearlessness comes from fear. The logic is quite simple. You might ask, for example, why someone takes a shower. You shower because you feel dirty. You aren't inspired to shower purely because you have clean clothes in your closet. We might say that basic goodness is like the clean clothes in your wardrobe. It's great to know that they are there, but it's not always enough motivation to get you to shower. The dirt is what really makes you want to clean up. Similarly, fearlessness comes from fear.

Being fearless is first of all, quite simply, having less fear or experiencing the cessation of fear. When as warriors we experience doubt and fear, then by rousing both our mind and body so that they are joined together, a good dose of fearlessness comes into our state of mind and is reflected in our body as well. Then we can appreciate the basic goodness we possess.

The first stage of fearlessness contains a feeling of joy and re-laxation or well-being. From the goodness of simply being your-self, a quality of upliftedness arises, which is not overly solemn or religious. It is joyful to be in such good health, joyful to have such good posture, joyful to experience that you are alive, you are here. You appreciate colors and the temperature of the air. You appreciate smells and sounds. You begin to use your eyes, your ears, your nose, and your tongue to explore the world.

You have never seen such penetrating and extraordinary red before. For the first time, you see such cool and beautiful blue. For the first time, you see such warm and delicate yellow. You see such refreshing, earthy, and wet green; such pure, clean white, as though you are opening your mouth and breathing out at the same time. For the first time, you see such wonderful black. It's so trustworthy that you can almost sleep on it. It has a sheen, which reminds you of stroking a black horse.

We can expand this to include the rest of our sense percep-tions: sound, smell, taste, and touch. Everything comes with a sense of appreciation. How wonderful the world is! How beauti-ful the world is! How exotic and how fabulous the world is! You might take the world for granted, but if you look again, you will find that tremendous beauty and subtlety exist in perception. You begin to feel almost as though you have been born again, or truly born for the first time. There is such pleasure and appreciation.

The warrior's virtue or decency comes from this basic sense of well-being, free from any neurotic or habitual preoccupa-tions. Decency here expresses a sense of joy, the joy of living, the joy of being alive. So there is more to fearlessness than merely having overcome fear. Beyond that, when we speak of fearlessness, we are describing a positive state of being full of delight and cheerfulness, with sparkling eyes and good posture.

This state of being is not dependent on any external circumstance. If you can't pay the electric bill, you might not have hot water in your house. The building you live in may not be well insulated. If you don't have indoor plumbing, you may have to use an outhouse. Millions of people in the world live this way. If you can raise good posture in your head and shoulders, then regardless of your living situation, you will feel a sense of joy. It's not any kind of cheap joy. It's individual dignity. This experience of joy and unconditional healthiness is the basic virtue that comes from being what we are, right now. You have to experience this natural healthiness and goodness personally. When you practice meditation, that brings the beginning of this experience. Then, when you leave the meditation hall and go out and relate with the rest of reality, you will find out what kind of joy is needed and what kind of joy is expendable. The experience of joy may be a momentary experience, or it could last a long time. In any case, this joy is an eye-opener. You are no longer shy of seeing the world. You find that the joy of warriorship is always needed.

In the midst of joy, your memory of fear may come up again. However, you are able to ride that fearful state of mind, whatever it may come from. So the second stage of fearlessness is being able to connect with or ride one's own mind properly. From that, the last stage of fearlessness is that you can steer your mind in whatever direction you want to go, into whatever area you want to explore and perceive.

Fearlessness is not like a wild tiger or brown bear that is locked up in a cage and growls every time you open the door. Fearlessness is powerful, but it also contains gentleness and constant loneliness and sadness. Wisdom and consideration for others are also part of fearlessness. When you are more fearless, you become more available and kinder to others, more considerate of others and more touched by them. The more fearlessness evolves, that much more available and vulnerable you become. That is why sadness and gentleness are part of fearlessness.

The joy of fearlessness brings the sadness. Joy doesn't stay by itself. If it did, there would be something wrong, something perverted about it. Real fearlessness is like mixing sweet and sour together. The tone of joyful sadness is like the sound of a flute, which is so melodic and beautiful. It ravishes your mind. It is not accompanied by any other musical instruments. The solo melody of the flute brings the echo of emptiness into your mind.

Such loneliness is almost romantic, as if you were in love. You think you might be falling in love, but you don't know with whom. You are in love without a particular object in mind. Such sadness is very soft. It's not a miserable sadness, but it feels sad because it is soft and pliable.

In this state, your mind doesn't buck like a young horse. Your mind is flowing like a gentle brook. There is only one brook in each valley, so the brook is all alone, making its gossipy little sound as it runs over the rocks. That kind of sadness and gentleness is synonymous with warriorship and fearlessness, which make life worthwhile.

This experience brings sympathy toward the world, including the world of the setting sun. The sadness you experience, as well as a sense of delight, encourages you to share your experience with others. You want to include them in your vision. You want to work with others and help them as much as you can. Confused existence, samsara, is not regarded as something that we have to attack, nor do we regard confusion as a disease that we should stay away from. Of course, if you are not very strong, you might have to stay away from the most confused experiences for a while, so that you won't be overly influenced by the neurosis of the setting-sun world. But when sadness and fearlessness are strong enough, you should look into how people in the setting-sun world conduct themselves.

People who have experienced the Great Eastern Sun are constantly gentle and fearless, whereas those who are still trapped in the world of the setting sun are aggressive and fearful. Whenever genuine sadness attempts to enter their minds, they try to block it from happening. To counteract the feelings of sadness and emptiness, people seek entertainment to distract themselves. This world of entertainment is designed to help you forget who you are and where you are. The setting-sun version of enjoyment is to forget your gentle sadness and instead become aggressive and "happy."

However, what you're experiencing is neither real happiness nor enjoyment. This perverse notion of happiness is based on forgetting that you exist, forgetting that your mind and body could ever be synchronized. Such a notion of happiness is based on separating mind and body altogether. You try your best to do this by putting your mind on a TV screen while your body is slouched in a chair. That's the closest to magic that exists in the setting-sun world. All sorts of entertainments have been developed so that your mind is kept away from your body. The objective here is completely the opposite of joining heaven and earth. Joining heaven and earth is not separating this and that, but making them indivisible. That unity or harmony is "it" or "That" with a capital *T*, without qualifications.

Ordinarily, people have many difficulties in relating to the world, which manifest in the form of passion, aggression, and ignorance—and this is far from being able to join heaven and earth. Nevertheless, working with others, regardless of their attitude, is still very important. The approach of the warrior in working with the setting-sun world is like an autumn leaf floating down a river. It doesn't change its color, and it doesn't struggle with the river. It goes along with it. This has a natural effect, because the brook or the river has never carried such an autumn leaf before. The setting-sun world will be uncertain what to do with this leaf. So by simply being there, you make people think twice, automatically.

It takes people off guard when you don't react to them. You don't fight back when they attack you, but you just remain as an autumn leaf, whatever they do. This is the gentle way of working. If there are hundreds of thousands of autumn leaves coming down a small brook, then the appearance of the brook will be changed by them altogether. The joke is on the people who are living in the world of the setting sun, and they have to think twice. They might smile and pretend to laugh, but behind that really they will be crying, weeping. So you see, an autumn leaf has a great deal of power over the world of the setting sun. Such little leaves could stop the flow of water altogether. If there are enough powerful autumn leaves, that is possible. It has been done in the past.

Working with others in this way, one is able to work with oneself at the same time. One's appreciation of the world never diminishes. When you open your eyes early in the morning, you don't say, "Oh, here's another day, another pain." First, you hear the rustling of the sheets on your bed. You feel your hair lying on your pillow, if you have any hair. In any case, you feel your head lying on the pillow, and you begin to look around, and you see the walls in your bedroom. That's where the delight begins to happen, from the first moment when you wake. There's a feeling of beauty and sensuality, almost as if you were in a royal palace. You think about what you're going to have for breakfast and what you're going to wear that day. Every decision becomes part of a celebration rather than purely a hassle. You feel that you are a complete human being. You don't feel that you are still dragging your umbilical cord with you throughout your life. Instead, you are a wholesome, complete, and independent human being.

Those qualities of celebration, dignity, and goodness provide almost a quality of worship in your life. From that, you discover the principle of the ruler in your life, being the king or queen in your own life. The Great Eastern Sun king or queen sits on the throne of exertion and wears the crown of patience. A setting-sun king would sit on the throne of laziness, wearing the crown of aggression and authority alone. The Great Eastern Sun ruler holds the scepter of mercy and genuineness, whereas the ruler of the setting sun carries the scepter of deception and ungenuineness.

There are two situations of ruling. One is personal: ruling one's own household. You and your partner or your friends or roommates could set up such a kingdom. Beyond that, there is a larger vision of enlightened society, in which the whole country or even the whole world is ruled on the basis of joining heaven and earth.

The ruler of the Great Eastern Sun views the world, the entire universe, with panoramic vision. He or she sees what needs to be done, what needs to be conquered, what needs to be overcome, what needs to be destroyed, what needs to be cherished. When you join heaven and earth, you experience total unity, a total sense of *That* which is unshakable. You cannot be disturbed by cowardice of any kind at all. You are there, right there. You are riding your mind, and the rider and what is ridden are the same thing. They are one piece. It is the complete synchronization of body and mind.

13

Making Friends with Fear

WE ARE DISCUSSING HOW to benefit others by joining heaven and earth, while fulfilling our own wishes and developing a perfect notion of warriorship. Because you are a warrior, fulfilling your wishes arises in the context of not harming others, not taking advantage of others, and not causing suffering to oneself or others. We have already talked about the basic virtue or decency of warriorship that arises from fearlessness and how that allows you to appreciate the world around you. We have also discussed the possibility of waking up our basic instinct toward unconditional goodness. Such goodness is neither good nor bad in the conventional sense. It is based on reawakening your own basic nature.

The expression of basic goodness is our next topic. This principle is known in Tibetan as *Ashe* (pronounced ah-SHAY). *A* means "first" or "primordial." *She* means "stroke" and also "life strength." So Ashe is the primordial stroke or strength of life. It can also mean "power" or "storehouse of power." Such power is not the gift of any external agents. It is reawakened power that exists naturally. Fire has power of its own. Wind has power of its own. Earth has power of its own. Space has power of its own. Such power has neither beginning nor end, and such power exists in you, individually, inseparable from basic goodness.

Sometimes the Ashe is referred to as a razor knife. Basic

goodness can't be too naive. It has its own strength, which is the quality of cutting through unnecessary neurosis. If you're bringing up a child and you love that child, sometimes you have to be sharp with him or her. Sometimes you say yes and sometimes you say no. On the whole, your purpose is to be good to your child. Similarly, the Ashe principle manifests basic goodness through its strength and the power of cutting through. This allows us to be clear, precise, and boundless in our vision.

The strength of basic goodness allows us to remain good, as we are, in the face of attacks of all kinds against this goodness. One of the greatest examples of the strength of basic goodness is the experience of the Buddha at the time of his enlightenment. At the very moment of his enlightenment, many evil forces attacked the Buddha, but he remained pure and in a state of tranquillity. *A* is that fundamental basic openness, that imperturbable and peaceful space. That is joined with the stroke or force of *she*. So Ashe altogether is the powerful existence arising out of basic goodness.

The Ashe principle has both relative and absolute aspects. Relative Ashe is connected with the fundamental principle of fearlessness. As we know, in order to understand fearlessness, one has to understand fear itself. Fear is a trembling, shaky feeling. Fundamentally, it is the fear of nonexistence.

Sometimes fear expresses itself in complete cowardice. When you are afraid, you may want to jump into somebody's lap or even hide in a pile of garbage, because at least that is reassuringly warm and smelly. Sometimes you might be so terrified that you can't even cry, and you lose any trace of a sense of humor. You lose your good posture and begin to hunch over like an animal. You begin to lose all the reference points that normally anchor your existence. You become empty-hearted, in a negative sense. You completely lose the quality of the monarch or ruler that we discussed in the last chapter.

Such fear is not necessarily problematic. It is like an attack of sneezing. It comes and goes. However, you have to study your fear. That is very important. You should have no problem discovering your fear. It is too obvious and visible. When you have a problem appreciating a chrysanthemum or the sunshine, that is a sign of fear. Because of your fear, you may lose your sense of humor, your sense of appreciation, and you may be blocking the vividness of your perceptions. You should see the vividness of the phenomenal world. When you are unable to do so, you need to develop mindfulness and awareness so that you can work with your fear. Study how fear arises, how it manifests, and how it is actualized. When you begin to understand your fear, then you find that it is almost a big joke rather than a big problem.

At that point, you shouldn't try to cast fear out. Instead, fear should be regarded as the kindling to build a big fire of fearlessness. You have to realize fear as the starting point of fearlessness. Fear is not regarded as black, and fearlessness is not regarded as white. You have to make friends with fear.

Fearlessness arises out of understanding fear. Step by step, you begin to understand why you are terrified of nonexistence, and at last you begin to understand fearlessness. At first there is a sense of relief, that you are finally looking into your fear and facing it. Then you develop inquisitiveness. You want to explore the whole area of fear. Having explored it, you can actualize real fearlessness. Such fearlessness is quite sharp, which is the principle of Ashe. The razor knife of Ashe cuts fear.

Then fearlessness dawns as a sense of humor or light touch. At that point, you remember that you are not just a frightened, solitary person. You remember that you live in a society. When we connect with other human beings, we touch into our creativity as human beings, and we begin to expand our world. That is the expression of fearlessness.

14

Monumental Nonexistence

THE PRINCIPLE of Ashe resides in your heart whether you are cowardly or brave. It is synonymous with basic goodness, and it is a manifestation of basic goodness. It is in our body, in our heart, in our brain, in our veins, in our blood, in our flesh. We all have the Ashe principle in us. It is the sense of constant magic that exists in us. That magic doesn't have to be sought for, but the magic is in us already. The only thing we have to do is to recognize it.

Although everybody has the Ashe principle in them, you must be introduced to the idea that such a thing exists in you. Then you can activate and proclaim it in your existence. So discovering the Ashe principle also brings a general sense of vision. You might be lost, roaming around in the wilderness, thinking that you're one of the apes. Then a human being comes up to you, taps you on your shoulder, and says, "Hey! You are not a monkey. You are a human being." At first you might be bewildered, but then you realize, "Ah! It might be true." Then you begin to make a fire, which monkeys don't do, and you cook food on the fire, which monkeys don't do. That's somewhat an analogy for this kind of transmission. It awakens you to a whole new dimension of your existence.

Realizing the Ashe principle in us brings an experience of brilliance and vitality. The term for that in Tibetan is *ziji*. *Zi* means "brilliance," and *ji* means "dignity"; so ziji is brilliance and dignity put together, which shines out. When you meet a friend who is in good health, you say, "You're looking good." The well-being you see in your friend is an expression of ziji. It could be regarded as basic charisma, although not in the style of a politician or a movie actor. It is a quality of basic health, which is good and definite. There is no tentativeness. It is solid, like a rock, but at the same time it is bouncy like a tiger. You are basically healthy and strong, so there is no room for sickness or obstacles to arise.

The way of the warrior is to reflect the brilliance of Ashe in body, speech, and mind. You have a good posture of upright head and relaxed shoulders. That doesn't cost you any money to achieve! Ziji is reflected throughout your appearance. You don't have to buy expensive clothes or get a fancy haircut. You can wear simple outfits, which still express your natural basic goodness. The whole approach is based on how you carry yourself and how you conduct yourself.

A warrior's speech is gentle but powerful. You don't slur your words. You pay attention to the vowels and consonants you are pronouncing, as well at to syntax and grammar. You proclaim yourself, whether you are talking to your two-year-old or fighting with your partner. The warrior's way is to pay attention to communication thoroughly, whether you are talking to a university professor, a bank manager, a taxi driver, a bus conductor, or a garbageman, or whether you are asking somebody for directions. The warrior's speech is never sloppy.

As far as the discipline of mind is concerned, you should rest your mind in basic goodness and appreciate that. Appreciating goodness brings a sense of celebration. Your world might be falling apart, you might be in tremendous financial debt, your husband or wife might be leaving you, or you might be living in a depressed neighborhood where the police sirens keep you awake at night. In spite of all these problems, if you appreciate being a Shambhala warrior, that inner glow of warriorship will help you. Think of the Ashe principle, the razor knife that cuts aggression; and think of basic goodness, which creates constant upliftedness. Those principles are not mere theory or concept. Sadness and joy are one in basic goodness. Don't try to push out the nightmare, and don't try to bring in the bliss. Just rest your being in a state of basic goodness. If necessary, you can actually say to yourself: "Basic goodness." It will help.

Up to this point we've been exploring Ashe in the relative sense, how it manifests in our ordinary, everyday experience. At the absolute level, the Ashe principle is nonexistence, which here means being vacant or empty of duality. It is just open space. In the Buddhist tradition, nonexistence is referred to as shunyata. *Shunya* means "empty," "not," or "no." *Ta* makes it "empti*ness*," "no-ness," or "nonexistence." Nonexistence is always in the background. Either it can be covered up or it can manifest, which allows us to work with this and that, good and bad, in the relative sense.

In the Buddhist tradition, as we have discussed, we talk about vajra nature, which is the diamond-like quality of nonexistence that is absolutely indestructible. It does not have any bias toward good or bad. Similarly, the absolute Ashe principle is described as being like a diamond and impossible to destroy. You cannot wound or slash space no matter how sharp your sword may be.

In the English language we talk about the hard truth, the hard facts of life. The Ashe principle is the hard facts and the hard truth that cannot be altered. There is nothing mystical about it. If you want to grasp it, it is simple, open, and intangible, but it is very much there. It is no longer regarded as a fanciful, mystical experience. The Ashe is in you; it is in the cosmos. It is universal. It is *That*. It arises in the form of a razor knife that cuts dualistic preoccupations and concepts of any kind. On the whole, this principle of basic goodness is non-ego, nothing to dwell on anywhere, but utterly sharp and superbly immovable and steady. It is monumental nonexistence. It is the essence of joining heaven and earth.

Part Three

RIDING THE ENERGY OF WINDHORSE

A windhorse is a special kind of horse. Horses are wonderful animals. Any sculpture of a horse is a sacred symbol. Horses represent the wild dreams that human beings would like to capture. The desire to capture any wild animal or to capture the wind, a cloud, the sky—all those are represented by the image of the horse. If you would like to ride on mountains or dance with waterfalls, all of that is incorporated in the symbolism of the horse. The actual physique of the horse—his neck, ears, face, back, muscles, hooves, tail—is the ideal image of something romantic, something energetic, something wild, which we would like to capture. Here, the horse is used as an analogy for that energy and all of those dreams.

15

Unconditional Confidence

AT THIS POINT, we are ready to talk about how we can work with others and communicate the essence of the Shambhala teachings to them. The point is not to convert anyone to our view, but rather to help people wake to their own view, their own sanity. Practically speaking, how can we do that? We have to go back to the beginning and take another look at our journey on the path.

Our opinions and attitudes about ourselves are very important. We cannot ignore the slightest tendency to feel wretched, inadequate, or fundamentally distrustful of ourselves. Those feelings always show through. This doesn't mean that you are not allowed to think anything bad about yourself. However, there is another side to you that is an expression of goodness. That has to be recognized as well. Otherwise, without that nature of goodness, the human race wouldn't be here at all. We would have destroyed ourselves a long time ago.

We have made our journey, we have gotten this far, and we can go on. That's basically what we call the Great Eastern Sun view. There's nothing particularly glamorous about it. It is a simple attitude. Beyond that, we have the interest or the desire, as well as the ability, to continue this journey. There is a spark that exists within us that allows us to feel healthy, together, and good.

What are we going to do with this sense of friendliness to ourselves? How does it affect our lives or the lives of others? When we have a feeling that life is worthwhile and we are worthwhile, from that, a sense of softness or gentleness begins to develop.

It is like watering the seeds in a garden. In this case, the gentleness that develops is like the moisture that helps a seed to grow so that greenery will unfold and flowers will blossom. Then, beyond that, you develop confidence. In this case, we are talking about unconditional confidence. The ordinary sense of confidence is confidence about something, which is conditional or qualified. But in this case, gentleness and softness give rise to an unconditional feeling that is awake, brilliant, and warm. When we have both moisture and warmth, we know that the plant will definitely grow. That confidence is the seed that we should share with the rest of the world.

Unconditional confidence is the pragmatic aspect of tenderness or gentleness. It is the action arising from the softness. Developing confidence is like watching the sun rise. First it seems very feeble and one wonders whether it will make it. Then it shines and shines. Confidence is not about arrogance or pride. It is a natural unfolding process. It's not a question of needing confidence or not needing it. It's naturally there. In fact, we actually don't have to develop confidence. It's more that we have to *acknowledge* the confidence that already exists.

If we want to present this unconditional confidence to others, to help others appreciate this quality in themselves, we don't have to be pedantic or heavy-handed. Confidence is there. It is a fact. It is the case. But surprisingly, nobody noticed it before. So telling people about this state of being is simply telling the truth. You don't have to make up anything at all.

This unconditional confidence manifests in our lives as appreciation: appreciation of our intelligence, our sympathy toward ourselves and others, appreciation of good food and drink, appreciation for our meditation practice. Appreciating the details of life begins to open up our life so that it is no longer purely a struggle but a jolly good life.

So the real way to share our understanding with others is to cheer ourselves up to begin with. Then, when we communicate with others, it should be very moving. Tenderness is based on touching the aspect of ourselves that is positive but at the same time slightly sad. We are talking about a human situation and how to feel like a human being. The humanness that exists within us is perhaps like a woman's womb, which is very sensitive and which nurtures life and is capable of giving birth. The heart of the Shambhala approach is this fertile gentleness. From that space you can wield the Great Eastern Sun. Because you are so human, you could be almost superhuman. But first we have to start with the humanness. One of the biggest problems in the world is that people don't feel themselves properly. So we are simply trying to feel ourselves, appreciate ourselves. The whole presentation of the way of the warrior is based on this gentleness.

Acknowledging that human beings possess goodness is the starting point. Otherwise we may indulge in our wretchedness or invite depression. We may turn away from ourselves, rather than being fully genuine. On the other hand, refusing to be a simple human being and trying to always be superhuman, not recognizing our basic human situation with all its difficulties and contradictions, is another way of being ungenuine. In either case, we are trying to be somebody or something else, and we're not paying attention to what's happening in our lives. We often invent and substitute somebody else for ourselves, some mythical person who doesn't even exist. Then we fail to find our own human quality, and we run into a lot of trouble. When you are being genuine, that state of being is indestructible. It depends on how much you can be a warrior.

16

Discovering Windhorse

IN THE LAST CHAPTER we discussed the importance of genuineness, truly feeling oneself as a human being. From that, you begin to realize that there is no fundamental problem with your human existence. Nothing about you needs to be destroyed or razed; no warfare is necessary. That, as we discussed earlier, is the ultimate idea of warriorship: being all-victorious. If you have to fight, you are not all-victorious. When you are all-victorious, you don't have to conquer anything. That's the attitude that we take here toward ourselves. Recognizing the goodness of human life is not based on suppressing or overlooking negativity, however. Rather, if you look at your experience and your mind, and you trace back through the whole process of your life, of who you are, what you are, and why you are in this world, if you look systematically, step by step, you won't find even a little drop of any problem at all.

If you take the Great Eastern Sun approach, the world hangs together already, and there isn't much room for chaos at all. Again, it's not a matter of *believing* in goodness. Rather, if you actually look, if you take your mind apart, your whole being apart, and examine it, you find that you are genuine, along with the rest of existence. The whole of existence is well constructed, and there's no room for mishaps of any kind.

Out of that, a further sense of healthiness or wholesomeness arises. Physically, psychologically, domestically, spiritually, you feel that you are leading your life in the fullest way. You feel gut-level wholesomeness, as if you were holding a solid brick of gold, which is heavy and substantial and shines with golden color. The situation feels not only real but also quite rich.

Movement or energy arises from that bank of richness. That energy is quivering, because it is so alive, so awake, and it begins to radiate out, making a journey back and forth to communicate or relate with the phenomenal world, your world. Normally, when a person projects energy, he tries to use that process of projection to fulfill his desire or to confirm his expectations. That produces a gap or a break, which subverts the wholesomeness. Doubt often arises at that point. You can catch all kinds of psychological fevers or flus in the gap of unhealthiness, and you may also communicate that unhealthiness back to the rest of your world.

In the true human situation, which is the situation of warriorship, we shouldn't have that problem. Rather, we expand and extend ourselves fully to a situation, and from that we receive the feedback to develop a true and clear understanding. There is no doubt about anything. Overall, the warrior's doubtlessness comes from continually connecting back with the original feeling of being truly oneself. From that, tremendous health can be propagated.

At this point, we refer to the Great Eastern Sun as the *Golden Sun of the Great East*, which refers to this quality of healthiness. Having uncovered this in ourselves, we might have a tendency to try to immediately convert people to our own healthiness, which is a mistake if we don't really know what we're doing. We may have experienced something that we can't even put our finger on, and although the experience may have been very powerful, nothing much happens when we try to communicate it to others prematurely. The only thing that really happens is that we contract mental and emotional sicknesses from others and become subject to their problems.

Genuine communication with others has to be a slow and organic process, which begins with ourselves. If we work with ourselves properly and thoroughly, then we can project wholesomeness effortlessly and naturally. This is not yet the experience of being a warrior completely, but just touching the essence or the seed of warriorship.

Naturally existing interest in the world is part of the Great Eastern Sun vision. Even though you might be doing something quite repetitive, like working in a factory or at a fast-food restaurant, whatever you are doing, you find that every minute of every hour is a new chapter, or at least a new page, in your life. A warrior doesn't need television. A warrior doesn't need comic books to entertain himself or be cheerful. The world that exists around the warrior is fully what it is, and the question of entertainment doesn't even arise.

Ordinarily, inquisitiveness comes from boredom, trying to occupy your time with something interesting. Or, if you are afraid, you may employ inquisitiveness to help you find a safe haven to protect yourself from whatever threat exists. For the warrior, inquisitiveness arises spontaneously and comes with a sense of raw delight. It is soft and tough at the same time. Sometimes, when you are delighted about something, you develop a thick skin and you feel smug. You think, "I am delighted." It's self-affirmation. But in this case, there's a touch of pain, which is not negative but just a touch of soreness or rawness. Whenever there is interest, you reflect back to the fundamental sadness and tenderness, which then allows you to project further genuineness, which in turn sparks further interest. At this point, you feel that your life is constantly moving forward.

So the logic of the Great Eastern Sun has a lot of psychological subtleties to it. Sometimes we refer to the *way* of the Great

Eastern Sun. The vision of the Great Eastern Sun provides a path for us. When you look at the sunrise, you may see beams or rays of light coming toward you. This is an analogy for the pathway of wakefulness and gentleness that is provided by the vision of the Great Eastern Sun, which is inviting you to walk on the path of the warrior. Unless you experience this personally, you cannot share this journey with anyone else.

Great Eastern Sun vision is also connected with the concept of windhorse, or *lungta* in Tibetan. Windhorse is a sense of gallantry, cheerfulness, upliftedness, and gentleness—all bundled into one state of being in the person of the warrior. Windhorse is a particular kind of magic that you discover when you connect with the principle of Ashe, or primordial confidence. The principle of Ashe actually sparks or ignites energy within the warrior, making him or her into almost a superhuman person. The way you carry yourself changes. You actually begin to look different. You begin to develop tremendous strength and elegance, which we have described earlier as ziji. Windhorse is tapping into the fundamental energy of Ashe; ziji is the product of windhorse. An analogy for this would be driving your car on the highway. Ashe is the engine, lungta is the gasoline that powers the car, and ziji is the speed you achieve traveling on the road.

To be elegant, you don't have to wear the latest fashions or have your suits custom-made. Elegance is not based on eating in the most expensive restaurants, driving the fanciest cars, or speaking with a certain pronunciation or an air of sophistication. Many people have tried to achieve elegance in those ways, if they could afford it. Those who couldn't often felt bad because, as they saw it, looking good was a matter of money. But in this case, the case of the warrior, you don't have to be extravagant. You can get something from the thrift shop, and when you put it on, it looks terrific, not because you're smart about putting certain combinations of clothing together but because you've developed windhorse.

Windhorse arises in the environment of Great Eastern Sun vision, which creates an atmosphere of sacredness in which you are constantly moving forward and recharging your energy. You feel that you are truly leading your life in the fullest sense. Then, you don't need an architect or a tailor to redesign your world for you. At this point, a further sense of warriorship takes place: becoming a real warrior.

All of this is part of what we call the warrior's meekness. By meek here, we don't mean being submissive or easily taken advantage of. Rather, meekness refers to the warrior's genuineness. Your life feels wholesome because you have been so thorough and methodical in examining your whole being. This basic experience is the foundation for the whole Shambhala path. Otherwise, the discussion of the Shambhala world may feel like it's purely presenting a myth. You might as well be watching a movie about Shangri-la, which is somewhat corny and convincing but completely made up.

When we talk about elegance, we are not talking in terms of arrogance. When we talk about fearlessness, we are not talking about heavy-handedness. Genuineness is different from trying to convince ourselves that something is there when it doesn't exist. Gentleness doesn't mean being polite and putting on the false mask of a bodhisattva.

Windhorse arises in the basic atmosphere of awareness and mindfulness. Out of that space of basic, constant sanity, a spark of delightfulness or a sudden flash of wakefulness can take place. This happens over and over again in your life. In the course of a day, you might descend into an almost subhuman level of doubt and depression and then bring yourself back to the level of warriorship over and over, throughout the day. The key to cultivating windhorse is the practice of meditation. On top of that, you make a connection to the principle of Ashe, or primordial wakefulness. Finally, your whole life is occupied or filled with the atmosphere of genuineness, and flashes of wind-horse can take place all the time.

Windhorse could be described as a bank or storehouse of energy, which is the product of genuineness. If you're a beginning warrior, first you have a flash of genuineness. Then, having recognized your genuineness, you automatically experience health and wholesomeness. Finally, you feel the spark or the wind of lungta, windhorse. In a fully developed warrior, that process happens all at once, but we can talk about it in stages.

Everything reverts back to being genuine. Whenever there's a gap, the only way to be a warrior is to refer back to the genuineness, which is somewhat raw and so tender and painful. That is the saving grace or the safety precaution, so that the warrior never goes astray and never grows a thick skin.

Discovering windhorse is really just a question of giving up your resistance, rather than working too hard to understand or finalize something. It's very simple and raw. Japanese koto music has these qualities of rawness and genuineness, musically speaking. Occasionally, people are afraid to recognize these qualities, which is an expression of their cowardice. If we don't understand ourselves, then we cease to be genuine and we lose everything that comes out of being genuine. You become unhealthy and you lose your windhorse, your lungta. Not knowing the nature of fear, you can't go beyond it. But once you know your cowardice, once you know where the stumbling block is, you just have to climb over it—maybe just three and a half steps.

17

The Spark of Confidence

THERE IS A DIFFERENCE between the amateurish warrior and the genuine warrior, which we could discuss in connection with the union of the secular and the spiritual. These subjects go hand in hand. A secular approach refers to looking directly at ourselves and discovering our existence, our health, and our glory without being influenced by a religious outlook. We're not particularly talking about the secular as something desecrated. You have your own resources and existence, and you simply embrace whatever is there to be discovered.

We might find that these "secular" experiences coincide with spiritual discoveries on the Buddhist path. We definitely are using the discipline of mindfulness and natural exertion to open to ourselves and constantly check up on ourselves, so to speak. In some subtle way, we might find that the secular becomes very sacred, very real and genuine. From that point of genuineness where the secular becomes sacred, we begin to discover the true warrior, the genuine warrior, as opposed to the mimicking or amateurish warrior.

At this point, we might discuss a little more about how we can work with other people and perhaps help them to wake up. We have developed our own discipline and understanding of fearlessness, but how can we share that with others? Metaphorically speaking, there are all sorts of extreme ways of waking others: knocking on their doors, shouting, pouring cold water on them—all sorts of ways of waking people up. Most of us have tried those ways of communicating with others in our life, as well as pounding on their heads and overwhelming them. When we use too much force without enough basic authority, or presence, then the joke will be on us. Things will bounce back on us. A genuine warrior wouldn't act in this way at all.

If your basic approach to communication is to get exasperated with people, as though you are tearing yourself to shreds on stage in front of an audience, some people might be convinced by your performance. If the audience is gullible enough, this technique might work. This has been done quite successfully by some people in the past. This is often the approach of charlatan teachers. However, when you have already discovered and connected with your own genuineness, a display like this won't work. It will backfire on you. That is the warrior's saving grace. It's a natural protective mechanism that makes it impossible for the true warrior to con others successfully.

There's only one way a true warrior can project to others: through personal understanding. Then you can demonstrate to people that their poverty-logic about their lives does not hold truth. Let them wake that way.

A genuine warrior has a lot of resources within herself, resources that are always there. Although you feel that you've run out of ideas, you're not really running out of anything. You're being attacked by your own cowardice. You can go beyond that and find further resources within yourself. Banks and banks of inspiration unfold constantly.

The magical trick or practice, the key to relating with others, is to project the physical and psychological healthiness of lungta, or windhorse. You might have had a terrible day, but when you turn your mind to communicating with others in the Shambhala style, you tune yourself in to lungta. You feel good, healthy, and ready to launch.

It is at this point that we have to be very careful that we're not purely trying to mimic windhorse, which is a bit tricky. Especially if you are facing a big challenge, such as giving a public presentation, asking someone to marry you, asking for a divorce, or asking your boss for a raise, you might have a tendency to artificially puff yourself up. Mimicking is conning yourself by saying "I'm going to do this, whether I feel real confidence happening or not." You have understood a few bits of simplistic logic and made a few notes, and you try to use those tricks to overwhelm others. Mimicking can't be bothered with genuine discipline or technique. It is being very pushy, very numb and heavy-handed. People are not going to be inspired by you strong-arming them. Nothing will come of it, because you haven't actually tuned in to the spark of windhorse at all.

Confidence comes from nowhere. It just arises. It's a sudden flash that has a very healthy note. Before you have to present yourself to others, you could spend at least five or ten minutes tuning in to confidence. Sit in a chair or on a meditation cushion and tune in to the giant ocean of healthiness. Then, when a spark of confidence arises, let it project out. Then there is no problem. Genuine communication is based on tuning in to the spark of confidence, which contains all the elements of wakefulness and power that we have been discussing. All these principles are included in this spark, this one basic flash. It is spiritual as well as secular, all in one. That is what will catch people's attention. Through that, their wandering thoughts and their subconscious gossip can be stopped.

18

The Other Side of Fear

As A WARRIOR proceeds on the path, he or she may go
through phases of intense fear. Frequently, such fear comes
out of nowhere. It just happens; it just hits you. It may cause you
to question everything in yourself: everything you have studied,
everything you have learned and understood, as well as your general life situation. You feel the wretchedness of the world around
you, as well as within yourself.

These attacks of fear often happen after you have understood the Great Eastern Sun vision and the principle of unconditional confidence. When you have understood things
spotlessly, then this fear may arise. It is actually a further phase
in the development of confidence. You are about to discover
further confidence.

Fear arises in this way many times on the warrior's path. It
is a hallmark of your progress on the path. In the early stages
of the warrior's growing-up process, we feel no contradiction
between our understanding and our ability to apply what we
have learned. Logically, we understand the process, and expe-
rientially we can connect with windhorse. But each time we
take a further step, as we begin to discover a further stage or
challenge of warriorship, just as we are about to give birth to
further confidence, that breakthrough is preceded by a sense
of utter fear.

When this occurs in your life, you should examine the nature of fear. This is not based on asking logical questions about fear: "Why am I afraid?" "What is the cause of my fear?" It is simply looking at the state of fear or panic that is taking place in you. Just look at it.

For some people, fear has no logic. For certain others, it brings tremendous logic of this and that. There are infinite possibilities, so many ways to prove that one's fears are valid. We can always find good reasons to be afraid. But in this case, rather than taking an analytical approach to fear, you should just look at your fear directly. Then, jump into that fear. If you do that, the next thing you will experience is a sense of complete flop. Fear brings together a lot of intense energy. When you dive into it, you feel as if you have just pierced a balloon. Or it's as if you have just dived into ice water; there's a sudden coldness.

Then you will feel the tinge of sadness that we've been talking about over and over again. Beyond that, you may feel some continuing sense of isolation and uncertainty, which is the leftovers of the fear, but nevertheless, the quality of intense fear begins to subside, and your fear becomes somewhat reasonable and workable.

We're not talking about a big event that takes place in one afternoon. The journey of working with fear takes place slowly and repeatedly as you go along the path. You may have many reruns: big reruns and then smaller reruns. Each time you experience fear, you reexperience and reconnect with the whole idea of genuineness, further and more completely. Fear will definitely arise in your life. Therefore it's crucial to understand how to combat that fear by going further into it and then coming out. None of us should regard ourselves as being trapped. From this point of view, we are free. We can do what we want to do. That is one of the key attitudes we should adopt. Even if you experience great fear, you can go in and out of it. That can be done. That is taking an imperial attitude: it can be done, and we can do it. That sense of freedom and fearlessness is very important.

If you understand this, then you won't dwell on your fear. In some sense, when you realize your fear, you will have already come out on the other side. Going into your fear is like going through a fog. The key is whether you're regarding what you experience as simply something real or instead as monumental entrapment, imprisonment. If you panic further, you breed cowardice. If you don't descend into cowardice, then you just have an experience of fear. You can break through without being a coward, at that point. It's a matter of invoking fundamental windhorse. If you are able to join fear and uncertainty with genuine confidence, then you will come through to the other side.

Dealing with the two sides of the coin in yourself is difficult, but it can be done. You discover a further commitment to working with yourself on the warrior's path and a further feeling of connection in your life. At that point, you are actually witnessing the joining together of heaven and earth. Heaven means sanity, or a good and direct understanding. Earth is practicality. Joining them together means that practicality and sanity, or wisdom, are put together, so that we can actually transmit that sanity to others.

Another way of seeing this is that heaven is oneself and the other is earth. The joining of heaven and earth is oneself and other joining together in sanity. In the past, you may have felt as though there were some kind of missing link with the universe. Sometimes there was no earth; sometimes you had no heaven. Sometimes the two didn't come together properly. Now, finally, experience feels full and completely joined together. You rediscover the sense of healthiness, a strong, healthy state of both mind and body. Your attitude toward yourself and others begins to brighten up. Only then can you actually hold the universe in your hand.

19

Invincibility

AS WE NEAR THE END of our journey together, it is important to discuss how to actually maintain the Shambhala world in ourselves twenty-four hours a day, so that we don't just have theories about overcoming arrogance and developing confidence. How can we apply the insights we have had, so that there is a sense of continual practice taking place? Invoking windhorse and having the confident awareness of the Shambhala warrior are very important disciplines, but there's something else we need to cultivate, which is a constant experience or quality of sacredness in everyday life.

We talked about the basic discovery of sacredness earlier, in chapter 6. Here I would like to introduce a further way to cultivate unconditional sacredness. Problems, difficulties, and challenges may arise quite suddenly in everyday life. We may have a flash of doubt or pain or an attack of emotion. At that very moment, at the same time, we can also have a flash of the sacredness in whatever arises, a sudden awareness of unconditional sacredness. It is very important to actually practice this and maintain it. This is very similar to the spark of confidence we have already discussed, as well as the idea of realizing vajra nature and the vajra world. The cultivation of sacred world on the spot is the practice that allows all phenomenal experience to become part of a Shambhala mandala, or the basic enlightened structure of your life.

Sacredness is not just an idea. It is an experience. Having a realization of sacredness means that you experience an element of power and dignity in everything, including the ballpoint pen you are using, your comb, taking a shower, or driving your car. Such little details of life have an element of the bigger vision and dignity of warriorship in them. Heaven and earth are joining together in each moment, which is the essence of sacredness.

Even though you may feel that many situations in your life are difficult or even degraded, nevertheless the entire world still possesses the potential for intrinsic awareness. All kinds of challenges and frustrations come up in life. We have to recognize that such frustrations, challenges, and negativity always have an element of sacredness in them. Appreciating sacredness is appreciating the sky in which the Great Eastern Sun can be brought out. If there's no sky, you are trying to give birth to the Great Eastern Sun on a concrete wall. There's not much dignity in that.

First, there is the flash of sacredness. Then, if we explore further, we find that there is a sense of humor in sacredness. Humor in this case does not mean mocking the world, but discovering a quality of delight and a light touch. This understanding of sacredness can actually ward off attacks of fear and negativity. Our existence is fortified, so to speak, with a sense of appreciation and sacredness. If fear tries to latch on to us, it finds us very slippery and it falls off easily.

Sacredness also provides space or accommodation in our life. If we don't have a sense of space, we begin to feel claustrophobic, which invites attacks of negativity. Sacredness is a spark of accommodation and generosity that can evoke further sympathy for and understanding of the nature of the setting-sun or degraded world. It shows us both how much pain people experience in that world and how ugly the whole scene is. When you witness this, you can be very understanding, but you don't have to go along with the neurosis. It shouldn't make you depressed, particularly. You feel good that you are free of that world, and that you have alternatives to offer, which can free yourself and also help to free others.

You begin to see the ins and outs of the samsaric or setting-sun world very clearly because you and your world are so brightly lit up. Sacred space allows you to see the contrasts, between elegance and the lack of elegance, between confidence and cowardice.

It's like a bright light shining in a dark room. When you see bright light, you see the darkness around it at the same time, and the more darkness you see, that much brighter the light becomes. The reason the warrior is invincible is that he sees his opponent's world so clearly and thoroughly. Because he knows the other world so well already, therefore the warrior can't be attacked or challenged. Here, spaciousness makes you sympathetic to others but invincible at the same time. Invincibility doesn't have to be insensitive. Instead, because you are so sensitive, so raw and rugged, therefore you can be hard like a diamond at the same time.

At this point, the warrior is meek like a tiger, not like a pussy-cat. There's real heart to your meekness. Meekness can actually roar and proclaim. Being meek is not being overly cautious and afraid to make mistakes. You may encounter many problems, but they will correct themselves if you have a true connection to the sacredness of the world.

At the same time, the realization of sacredness brings further loneliness, that sad and tender feeling we have been discussing. It comes with a sense that only you know your world. You can express only so much to others. There are always aspects of your experience that you cannot share. It's a feeling of unrequited love. But that isn't a problem, particularly. Rather, it's the source of the sacredness. Tenderness balances your experience, so that you don't feel you are wearing a suit or armor and beating your chest. For the warrior, proclaiming your wisdom always comes along with softness and sadness.

20

How to Invoke Windhorse

WHAT INSPIRES Great Eastern Sun vision altogether is the notion of being delighted to be human beings. The rising sun has the qualities of an infant or teenage sun, whereas the Great Eastern Sun is the mature sun, the sun in the sky at about ten in the morning. We are delighted to be who we are and delighted by the situation we are in. We appreciate the coincidences that have led us to this point in our lives.

Having discovered the Great Eastern Sun, how can we fulfill that vision? The first step is just basic warriorship, appreciating who we are, what we are, where we are. Such appreciation and investigation may bring up fear and many questions. Fear becomes our study material, which in turn becomes our working basis. We begin to realize that we have no choice but to work with fear and then to step over our fear and hesitation. Because our journey is choiceless, we develop a further sense of warriorship. We actually identify ourselves as warriors, and beyond that, we become citizens of the Shambhala world, the warrior's world.

How do we proceed at this point on the warrior's path? The mechanism or technique that we use is to invoke windhorse, or lungta. The practice of windhorse is a way of casting out depression and doubt. It takes the form of a cheering-up process. That is to say, invoking windhorse actualizes the living aspect of fearlessness and confidence.

The process of invoking windhorse begins by taking your seat, taking your place in the warrior's world, the sacred world. It is finding the right place to be. Only you can choose the magical spot. This cannot be found by intellectual speculation or scientific research. You cannot use technology to locate the right spot. You simply take the attitude of your existence as a warrior. Having assumed the warrior's posture, you feel oriented to the world that surrounds you. East is where you are facing; South is to your right; West is to your back; North is on your left.

These are not geographical directions, nor is this sense of direction scientific. It is intuitive. For instance, if I am talking to someone, my East is coming toward them and their East is approaching me, so we meet in the East. Wherever there is a meeting place, it happens in the East, which we could call the Great East at this point. It is where forward vision takes place. That includes many human activities: eating, making love, walking. You are always going toward the East. You walk forward, usually; when you eat, your food is in front of you; when you talk to someone, you usually face them. That is the idea of forward vision.

Having assumed the magical spot, you should arrange the throne of the ruler. This is acknowledging that you are not invoking windhorse in isolation, but as part of a larger society. In order to have a society, there must be some sense of leadership. The ruler's throne symbolizes that. As a warrior, you belong to the people of the Great Eastern Sun. You are a citizen in that world. Connecting with this sense of larger community or society is arranging the throne of the king or queen. In your own life, you may be the ruler. In the greater society, you are an integral part of the whole mandala.

In the process of raising windhorse, the next step is to contemplate the Great Eastern Sun. Taking your place in the world produces an almost physical effect. A great deal of energy comes from that, and you begin to feel that you almost *are* the

Great Eastern Sun. You have a sense of radiance and brilliance. It's an almost dazzling experience. This might be prolonged or just a quick glimpse. When you feel this, you should just touch it. Touch on the energy, not indulging or exaggerating it. Just touch.

Then you feel that you are connecting with greater energy, something beyond your own personal existence or even your place in society. You feel that you are tapping into your heritage, the tradition of warriorship altogether. So at that point, you feel that you are welcoming the Shambhala lineage of warrior kings and queens and inviting them to witness, or even judge you, as you invoke windhorse. In other words, you feel that the experience is legitimate, that there is no phoniness at all. What you are doing is deliberate, precise, clear, and real. It might be empty, in the Buddhist sense that all experience is empty. Nevertheless, this is genuine emptiness, genuine and powerful imagination, or visualization, we might say.

Then, having prepared the ground and invited the guests or the witnesses, you are ready to actually invoke or raise windhorse on the spot. What we are invoking is a wind *horse*, which is a special kind of horse. Horses are wonderful animals. Any sculpture of a horse is a sacred symbol. Horses represent the wild dreams that human beings would like to capture. The desire to capture any wild animal or to capture the wind, a cloud, the sky—all those are represented by the image of the horse. If you would like to ride on mountains or dance with waterfalls, all of that is incorporated in the symbolism of the horse. The actual physique of the horse—his neck, ears, face, back, muscles, hooves, tail—is the ideal image of something romantic, something energetic, something wild, which we would like to capture. Here, the horse is used as an analogy for that energy and all of those dreams.

In the process of invoking windhorse, there are three stages. The first is having a *joyful mind, free from doubt.* When you ride on a horse, if you relax with the horse, you find that you are actually riding on top of the world. There is a sense of conquering and being conquered at the same time. At that very moment when you are on the horse, there is no sadness involved, and there is no doubt that you are on top of the universe, riding the world. Of course, at the same time, you have to pay attention to the reins, your posture, balancing your weight on the horse, and many other factors. Still, you have to admit that you are riding your own mind at its best. There is almost a military feeling of strength and presence about it, and maybe a regal feeling as well.

You are in contact with an entirely different energy. The horse and rider are different entities, obviously. You are human, and the horse is a horse. Nevertheless, some kind of connection can be made. When you are riding on the horse, you experience oneness, particularly if you are a good rider who is free from doubt.

The same thing applies to riding your own state of mind, your own state of being. There are doubts of all kinds: doubts about yourself, doubts about others, and doubts about the situation. As you ride your horse, you may have doubt about the horse, about the environment, and about your capability to ride that particular horse. Still, there is an overall sense of togetherness or oneness. Fundamentally being free from doubt can take place when you are properly mounted on the horse of mind.

The second stage of longing for the horse is having a *genuine mind of sadness*. Having overcome your doubt completely, at that point you are mounted on your horse and you feel *there*, right there. At the same time, there could be a little bit of frustration, wishing that you could go further. You wish you could ride the horse so well, so effortlessly, that you wouldn't even have to think in terms of riding at all, but you would just be working effortlessly with your own mind. The notion of sadness comes from frustration of that nature.

Your sadness is almost nostalgia, although that is not quite the right word. Nostalgia means longing for something in the past, but here it is nostalgia for the present taking place. It is heartache. You wish that you could impart all the things in your mind to somebody else. You wish you could completely communicate to somebody. Everybody wants to do that, particularly when they are in love, or when they are angry. But it is usually impossible. Such communication can only take place in gestures. There are a lot of things that words don't say. That is the biggest frustration of human beings.

When we talk about sadness here, we are talking in the context of our devotion to warriorship and the Shambhala world. We feel so much commitment to the heritage of sanity that has been shared with us, so much longing to express that. You would like to capture or embody the true, genuine, and enlightened warrior in your state of being. But you cannot do it completely.

This sadness also comes with joy. The joyful, uplifted, and almost arrogant experience of riding on this particular horse makes you feel so good. Yet the goodness is always tinged with sadness. This is genuine sadness as opposed to a performance of sadness or a sadness of desperation. Windhorse touches your heart because it is so real. When the warrior is in this state of mind, she begins to feel that she is flying a kite that soars in the air, while the cord is attached to her heart with a hook. So you ride your horse, flying your kite, with the hook at the end of the cord touching your heart.

Beyond that, the third stage of longing is being *suddenly free from fixed mind*. You are not looking back at all or trying to confirm anything. Free from fixed mind means that there is no feedback. You are not trying to build a case or a logic to confirm your experience. There is the powerful sense that you are experiencing the highest level of genuine sadness and joy without doubt. You have no subconscious gossip in your mind at all.

Your mind is completely stopped, just stopped, in the positive sense. The attempt to create subconscious mind would be problematic at that point. Therefore, the idea is to cut through that, in exactly the same way as we do in the sitting practice of meditation. We let go of thoughts, naturally and powerfully. Because you are fully there, completely there, there is no subconscious mind at all.

The fruition of invoking windhorse is symbolized by the universal monarch with a broken heart. Such a person is also humble because of his broken heart. He is a real person. But at the same time, there is a lot of presence, in the positive sense. The feeling of this state of being is like looking at where the horizon meets the ocean. You have great difficulty distinguishing exactly where the sea dissolves into the sky. So heaven and earth are one.

This is the best description of invoking windhorse that I can offer. You have to experience this. We can't really talk about it too much. In some sense, it's a physical experience, but on the other hand, it is also psychological. Having ridden such a good horse, you have glimpsed what it would be like to conquer the universe. This is not conquering the universe from the point of view of acquiring power and wealth and subjugating others. We are not talking about feeling good by imposing your power on somebody. This is more psychological. We are describing the ultimate experience of feeling wholesome and real. You have nothing else to conquer. You have conquered what needed to be conquered completely. Basic goodness, genuineness, and fearlessness all come from that.

Conclusion

IN ONE SENSE, our discussion here has been quite simple and reasonable. The proclamation of gentle sanity may seem straightforward and almost self-evident, but on the other hand, it is somewhat outrageous. The more you get into the wisdom of Shambhala, the more you realize the outrageous aspect of these teachings.

Without some experience of the sitting practice of meditation, you may find it difficult to develop much understanding of what I've been trying to say. And you might find it difficult to cultivate these teachings in everyday life. One of the best ways to develop and apply your understanding is through the sitting practice of meditation. It is a very important discipline to cultivate.

As you practice this discipline, you may see many problems in yourself and in society, but please don't reject yourself or your world. We talked earlier about the virtue of renunciation, but that doesn't mean that you should give up on this world. Renunciation here is renouncing a small-minded attachment to privacy. You can jump in and involve yourself in life. As you continue your life's journey through fear and fearlessness, please remember to appreciate your world.

You have to develop yourself first; then you can begin to work with others. In the Shambhala tradition we don't jump the gun, so to speak. As warriors, we don't put on a suit of armor to go into battle against the setting sun until we are sure that we ourselves are fundamentally strong, well trained, and in good health. Essentially, we know that we have unconditional confidence so that we can stand on our own, without any gadgetry. We also make sure that the tools we use and the armor we don are well made. The armor of gentleness and fearlessness fits us well and is completely broken in, so that it will work *with* us rather than against us.

Although our discussion of the development of human warriorship uses many colorful analogies of battle and warfare, being a warrior in the Shambhala tradition has nothing to do with the normal aggression and warfare in the world. The warrior is one who is brave enough to live peacefully in this world. Courage is needed at every stage of life. If for some reason a newborn infant is afraid to suckle at his mother's nipple, we have to help that infant to connect with his world. He needs to be a warrior so that he will not reject the source of nurturing in his world. So while being a warrior may have different connotations, the fundamental, basic definition is embracing goodness.

In talking about such seemingly advanced subjects as joining heaven and earth and raising windhorse, we should always remember that, in essence, these teachings are simply rousing our innate nature of goodness, which is completely without aggression. When there is aggression, you lose your confidence and energy. You become weak, stubbornly self-centered, and angry. When there is no anger, you can raise yourself up and you expand yourself. You find that life is full of humor and cheerfulness.

Authentic fearlessness arises from this connection with basic, unconditional *goodness*. By goodness here, we simply mean being yourself. Accepting yourself—rather than trying to be good by being solemn and religious about your behavior—leads to uplifted confidence in body, speech, and mind. When goodness and virtue are awakened through the sitting practice of meditation, you train yourself to have good posture and to harmonize your mind and your body. Then goodness or virtue develops naturally in your speech and throughout your life, and you find the genuine way of working with others.

Being genuine means not having aggression and being true to oneself. A lot of us feel attacked by our own aggression and by our own misery and pain. But none of that particularly presents an obstacle. What we need, to begin with, is to develop kindness toward ourselves, and then to develop kindness toward others. This approach may sound very simpleminded, which it is. At the same time, it is *very* difficult to practice.

Pain causes chaos, fear, and resentment, and we have to overcome that. It is an extremely simple logic. Once we can overcome pain, we discover intrinsic joy, and we have less resentment toward the world and ourselves. By naturally being here, we have less resentment. When we are resentful, we are somewhere else, because we are preoccupied with something else. Being a warrior is being simply here without distraction and preoccupation. And by being here, we become cheerful. We can smile at our fear.

So fearlessness is not the simpleminded product of overcoming or overpowering your fear. For the warrior, fearlessness is a positive state of being. It is filled with delight, cheerfulness, and a sparkle in your eyes. Mahatma Gandhi was an example of someone who embodied such virtue and fearlessness. Gandhi was totally committed to helping India become an independent nation. He embraced all the obstacles, all the problems, and he used every possible way to win independence without violence. In one's own life, one can apply a smaller version of that kind of courage. We can become fearless and genuine, gentle and daring. But to do so, we have to keep a sense of humor, always.

Whenever there is doubt, that creates another step on your

staircase. Doubt is telling you that you need to take another step. Each time there is an obstacle, you go one step further, beyond it, step by step. You walk or you jump one step at a time until you see the Great Eastern Sun. I wouldn't suggest that in the beginning you look at the Great Eastern Sun directly—the light might burn you—but I wouldn't suggest you wear sunglasses all the time either. In the shade of fearlessness, you can appreciate the light that comes from the Great Eastern Sun, and then you can appreciate how it illuminates the colors of everything around you. Then slowly but surely, you will actually see the Great Eastern Sun directly without its blinding you. That is the warrior's way, and that is the way that we can conquer fear.

You may feel lonely on your journey; still, you are not alone. If we sink, you and your warrior comrades and I will all sink together. If we rise, we rise together. So you have a companion, even if we never have met one another personally. In the Shambhala tradition, we cry a lot because our hearts are so soft. And we fight the setting sun because we feel that basic goodness is worth fighting for, so to speak. Our obstacles can be conquered. So we should cry and fight, as long as we know that the warrior's cry is a different type of cry and the warrior's battle is a different type of battle.

As a warrior without aggression, you are fearless and good. Fundamentally, you can never make a mistake, so please cheer up. Even in the darkest of the dark age, there is always light. That light comes with a smile, the smile of Shambhala, the smile of fearlessness, the smile of realizing the best of the best of human potential. All of the teachings, the very heart's blood of Shambhala, are yours. We are all part of the same human family. Let us smile and cry together.

Fearlessness and Joy Are Truly Yours

When a warrior king presents a gift,
It could be a naked flame, which consumes the jungle of ego,
Or an ice-cold mountain range, which cools the heat of
    aggression.
On the other hand, it could be a parachute.
One wonders whether it will open or not.
There is a further choice—Thunderbolt:
Whether you are capable of holding it with your bare hand is up
    to you.
So, my heartfelt child, take these gifts and use them
In the way that past warriors have done.

Editor's Afterword

Smile at Fear is the last of three volumes that presents the Shambhala teachings of Chögyam Trungpa Rinpoche. I worked on the first book, *Shambhala: The Sacred Path of the Warrior*, quite intensively with the author. It was the first time I served as the lead editor of one of Rinpoche's books for general publication. In retrospect, it's amazing that he trusted me to edit the material, as I was rather green and young for the task. I suppose, in a sense, that his students all were, in those days. Nevertheless, because of his genius and with his guidance and the feedback of many other people, that effort worked out all right. The book was published in 1984. It was well received, and it still is.

After his death in 1987, the success of the first volume gave me the confidence to edit some of the wealth of the remaining material for publication. With the support of Shambhala Publications, *Great Eastern Sun: The Wisdom of Shambhala* was published in 1999. I applied a lighter hand to the editing of that book, which I hope retains the energy of the original presentations.

Now, ten years later, *Smile at Fear* has been published. The theme of fear and fearlessness was first presented in *Shambhala*, and the association of fearlessness with a sad and tender heart is one of the often-remarked-upon themes from that volume. Over the years, I came to see that fearlessness was a component of the Shambhala teachings at every level and that Rinpoche had often identified it as the core or heart of the Shambhala teachings. I began to think about making the teachings on fear and fearlessness the focus of the final book. As events unfolded in the last ten years, it seemed that these teachings on fear and fearlessness were the very teachings that might be the most useful for this era. And coincidentally, many of them were from talks that had not yet been edited at all. As he did so often during his lifetime, Rinpoche seemed again to have known with uncanny foresight and accuracy what tools we would need, in order to work with twenty-first-century experience. He had embedded those tools—or weapons, as a warrior might call them—into the Shambhala teachings, so that they would be right at hand when they were required.

For this volume I have drawn on a great variety of material, as detailed in the Sources section. In consultation with my editor at Shambhala Publications, Eden Steinberg, I decided to take some risks with the editing in order to produce a coherent, continuous flow, so that the book would read as a unified whole rather than as a collection of talks or articles. I also edited with the aim of revealing as much as possible of the immediacy and heartfelt quality of these teachings.

In the preparation of all three books, I held in mind the instructions and the feedback that Chögyam Trungpa gave me directly about the first volume. (You can find a detailed discussion of this in the introduction to volume 8 of *The Collected Works of Chögyam Trungpa*. This introduction can be read online at: www.shambhala.com/html/new/specialoffers/trungpa/v8_intro.pdf.) The editorial approach I adopted for *Smile at Fear* was guided by Rinpoche's wish to reach out to as many people as possible with these books.

I have been cautious about adding my own words to the author's, but in places I found it necessary to insert a phrase of explanation or a sentence to create continuity in the argument.

I've also updated some references. For example, whereas Chögyam Trungpa in 1978 alluded to people going to Dairy Queen for entertainment, I substituted Starbucks. *Perambulator* was replaced by *baby stroller* and other Anglicisms were changed to American terms. Gender references were updated as well, which I think Rinpoche would have appreciated. He went out of his way a number of times in his Shambhala talks to make it clear that "warrior" was a term that applies equally to brave men and women.

Throughout his presentation of the Shambhala teachings, Rinpoche stressed the importance of meditation and how the understanding of and connection to the teachings arise from sitting practice. In some sense, the teachings unfold from the practice. Because his instructions for practice were unique and somewhat unusual, especially in the emphasis on the gap and identifying with the out-breath, I thought it important that his approach to meditation be clearly presented here.

A person could take a stab at practicing meditation purely based on reading these books. However, Rinpoche himself always emphasized the importance of receiving personal instruction in meditation. The Resources section gives information about centers where you can learn to meditate. For those who already have a background in meditation, I trust that Rinpoche's discussion of practice also will prove helpful. The view and details of any meditation practice will influence one's perception in everyday life as well as on the meditation cushion. I think that the connection between Chögyam Trungpa's unique approach to meditation and the profundity and immediacy of the Shambhala teachings was not just a coincidence.

Rinpoche's use of royalty as a recurring metaphor and symbol may feel anachronistic to some readers. It seeks to address the human aspiration for a good, uplifted, and fulfilling life. In the vajrayana tradition of Buddhism, the practitioner in some ceremonies receives a crown, a scepter, even a new name as part of the empowerment to begin a practice. This has similarities to Trungpa Rinpoche's introduction of the idea of ruling your world as a king or queen. He had a somewhat democratic view of monarchy, in that he felt that every human being can play this role in his or her own life. The ability to see people at their best reflects the sacred outlook that he brought to every moment and experience of life. He actually saw the people he worked with as potential royalty. I remember once hearing from some friends how Rinpoche had spent an evening describing each of them as they would appear *when* they became a buddha. Not if, but when.

Similarly, his use of the metaphor of the warrior arose from his own experience. He was intimately familiar with the way fear and fearlessness operate in life, and he genuinely wanted to share his understanding of how the experience of fear can help us to meet life's challenges with bravery, rather than to see fear as our enemy. This was obvious from the way in which he himself constantly took chances and also in how he encouraged his students to do the same. Encouraging me to be the editor of *Shambhala* is just one small example of how he trusted his students and pushed us to undertake things we might never have thought we were capable of, yet longed to do. This, I think, is one reason that so many of his students feel that they could never do enough to repay his kindness.

Acknowledgments

Many people helped to record and transcribe the material in *Smile at Fear*. In particular, Tingdzin Otro spent many hours transcribing previously unused material, after Gordon Kidd of the Shambhala Archives provided the tapes for transcription. Their efforts are greatly appreciated. Altogether the staff at the

Archives was generous in providing access to the extensive collections they preserve. Some of the material used here was previously recorded, transcribed, and, in some cases, edited for use in other contexts. Thanks to David Rome, Judith Lief, Sara Coleman, Helen Berliner, Barbara Blouin, Richard Roth, Paul Halpern, Robert Walker, Bruce Wauchope, Ned Nisbet, and others for these earlier contributions.

In 2001, following the events of 9/11, Melvin McLeod encouraged me to edit an article by Chögyam Trungpa on fear and fearlessness for the *Shambhala Sun* magazine. This led me to revisit a seminar from 1979. I reedited the material for the *Sun*, and this started me thinking about the book as a whole. (That article appears here as a core teaching.) I appreciate Melvin's role as muse for this material.

Many people at Shambhala Publications have played a part in the unfolding of these three books. Samuel Bercholz, the founder of Shambhala Publications and its editor in chief, supported the publication of all three volumes. His inviolable connection to the material has been an important underpinning. Hazel Bercholz designed two of the covers, bringing a powerful connection between appearance and meaning, which in part arises from the visual dharma that she studied with the author himself. Emily Hilburn Sell was the patient and insistent editor of *Great Eastern Sun*. Both her appreciation of the material and her critical feedback were invaluable. Eden Steinberg is the editor of *Smile at Fear*. She brings a fresh sensitivity to her reading of the material. She has a way of guiding the editorial process that is both light-handed and penetrating, and I always feel that her involvement improves the books we work on together. Peter Turner has also been encouraging in crucial ways. Kendra Crossen was the in-house editor of *The Collected Works of Chögyam Trungpa* and the freelance copyeditor for *Smile at Fear*. Her gentle, meticulous hand and penetrating eye improve everything she works on, in a way that is somewhat invisible but undeniable. I also would like to thank Jonathan Green, who works on the foreign rights, contracts, and permissions associated with all of Chögyam Trungpa's books. Thanks to Ben Gleason for editorial contributions and to Daniel Urban-Brown for the design of the book.

I would also like to thank the members of my family, who have supported my editorial work over the years in many ways, from relieving me of financial stress to the much more important psychological and spiritual support they have provided. In particular, I thank my parents, Edward and Evelyn Rose, now deceased; my husband, James, and my daughter, Jenny. In addition to my biological family, many thanks are owed to my dharma brothers and sisters, who have encouraged the work I do in many ways.

Rinpoche's family has been supportive of the publication of his work for many years, and I thank them all. The author's widow, Diana Mukpo, continues to encourage the publication of new work, and her keen oversight, her protection of the teachings, and her kindness and friendship to me have been of great importance. Rinpoche's eldest son, Sakyong Mipham Rinpoche, as Buddhist and Shambhala lineage holder, continues to present the Shambhala teachings of his father. His own teachings reflect this connection. I am grateful to him for his dedication and support. Trungpa Rinpoche's senior students support his legacy in myriad ways. And very importantly, new students continue to discover the work of Chögyam Trungpa and to benefit from the wisdom of Shambhala.

To Chögyam Trungpa himself, profound and brilliant teacher, I offer a deep Shambhala bow. May the world breathe the air of goodness and bravery that comes from your lips, dispelling the clouds of ignorance. May we see the smile of Shambhala, which is also your smile, on the faces of those we encounter. There are no adequate thanks for the gift of these teachings. May we apply them in life and in death, and may they save all sentient beings from the warring evils of the setting sun.

Carolyn Rose Gimian
Halifax, Nova Scotia

Sources

The epigraph on page v is a quotation from "Mirrorlike Wisdom," in *Great Eastern Sun: The Wisdom of Shambhala* (Boston: Shambhala Publications, 1999), p. 75. © 2001 by Diana J. Mukpo. Used by permission.

Part 1 is primarily based on "Warriorship in the Three Yanas," an unpublished seminar given at Rocky Mountain Dharma Center (now Shambhala Mountain Center), Red Feather Lakes, Colorado, August 22–27, 1978. Secondary sources include the "Dathun Letter," an unpublished article on meditation, put together from talks in the early 1970s and given to students beginning a dathun, or month-long meditation program; Talk One of "The Warrior of Shambhala" seminar at Naropa Institute (now Naropa University), Summer 1978; and Talk One of a seminar on meditation at Naropa Institute, June 12, 1974. Chapter 7, "The Education of the Warrior," is based on material in *The Collected Kalapa Assemblies: 1978–1984* (Halifax, Nova Scotia: Vajradhatu Publications, 2006), pp. 133–38. Used by permission. Chapter 8, "Nonviolence," was originally published as "The Martial Arts and the Art of War" in *The Collected Works of Chögyam Trungpa,* volume 8, pp. 413–19. © 2004 by Diana J. Mukpo. Used by permission.

Chapters 9–11 of Part 2 are reprinted and slightly reedited from the article "Conquering Fear," which appeared in the March 2002 issue of the *Shambhala Sun* magazine, pp. 26–33, 70–74. © 2002 by Diana J. Mukpo. Used by permission. It also appears in volume 8 of *The Collected Works of Chögyam Trungpa*, pp. 394–407. Chapters 12–14 were compiled and edited from unpublished talks given by Chögyam Trungpa within the Shambhala Training Program in 1982 and 1983. The various seminars were simply entitled Level B/F or Level F. They do not correspond to any nomenclature in use within that program today.

Part 3 is a newly edited version of talks given to directors of Shambhala Training in 1978.

The conclusion is based on material from Level B/F and Level Fs mentioned above, as well as a small amount of material excerpted from *Great Eastern Sun: The Wisdom of Shambhala*, © 2001 by Diane J. Mukpo. Used by permission.

"Fearlessness and Joy Are Truly Yours" is an excerpt from a longer unpublished poem written to the Vajra Regent Ösel Tendzin as a birthday greeting, composed on August 20, 1981.

Further Readings and Resources

Readings

Two additional books by Chögyam Trungpa on the Shambhala path of warriorship are *Shambhala: The Sacred Path of the Warrior* and *The Great Eastern Sun: The Wisdom of Shambhala*. A boxed set—*Shambhala: The Sacred Path of the Warrior, Book and Card Set*—includes a paperback edition of *Shambhala*, a small handbook, and a stack of slogan cards that can be used to contemplate these teachings on working with oneself and others.

Ocean of Dharma: The Everyday Wisdom of Chögyam Trungpa presents 365 short inspirational quotations from the work of Chögyam Trungpa. Additional discussion of the practice of meditation and an in-depth treatment of mindfulness and awareness meditation (shamatha and vipashyana) is provided by Chögyam Trungpa in *The Path Is the Goal: A Basic Handbook of Buddhist Meditation*.

Cultivating loving-kindness and compassion toward all beings is at the root of Chögyam Trungpa's approach to working with others. *Training the Mind and Cultivating Loving-Kindness* presents fifty-nine slogans, or aphorisms related to meditation practice, that show a practical path to making friends with oneself and developing compassion for others.

The Sanity We Are Born With: A Buddhist Approach to Psychology is an excellent overview of Chögyam Trungpa's writings on the Buddhist view of mind, the practice of meditation, and the application of the Buddhist teachings to psychology and solving psychological and human problems of self-doubt, depression, and neurosis. For readers interested in an overview of the Buddhist path, the following volumes are recommended: *Cutting Through Spiritual Materialism, The Myth of Freedom and the Way of Meditation,* and *The Essential Chögyam Trungpa.*

Chögyam Trungpa's teachings on applying a meditative approach to art and being artful in everyday life are presented in *True Perception: The Path of Dharma Art.* In this context, he presented a number of teachings related to the Shambhala path of warriorship.

Resources

Ocean of Dharma Quotes of the Week brings you the teachings of Chögyam Trungpa Rinpoche via the Internet. An e-mail is sent out several times each week containing an excerpt from Chögyam Trungpa's extensive teachings. Quotations are selected by Carolyn Rose Gimian from unpublished material, forthcoming publications, or previously published sources. To subscribe or to see the quotes online, go to www.oceanofdharma.com.

Shambhala International is a global community with more than 170 centers and groups around the world, as well as thousands of individual members. Shambhala Meditation Centers offer courses in mediation and other contemplative arts and disciplines. For information regarding meditation instruction, please visit the website of Shambhala International at www.shambhala.org. This site contains information about the centers affiliated with Shambhala. For publications from Shambhala International, including books and audiovisual materials, go to www.shambhalashop.com.

The Chögyam Trungpa Legacy Project supports the preservation, propagation, and publication of Trungpa Rinpoche's dharma teachings. This includes plans for the creation of a comprehensive virtual archive and learning community. For information, go to www.chogyamtrungpa.com. For information about the archive of the author's work, please contact the Shambhala Archives: archives@shambhala.org.

The *Shambhala Sun* is a bimonthly Buddhist magazine founded by Chögyam Trungpa Rinpoche. The magazine also contains a listing of centers that offer meditation programs and instruction in many Buddhist traditions, throughout North America. For a subscription or sample copy, go to www.shambhalasun.com.

Buddhadharma: The Practitioner's Quarterly is published four times each year. A listing of meditation centers offering instruction can be found in the journal. For a subscription or sample copy, go to www.thebuddhadharma.com.

About Chögyam Trungpa

BORN IN TIBET IN 1940, Chögyam Trungpa Rinpoche was recognized in infancy as an important incarnate teacher. His was the last generation to receive the complete education in the teachings of Buddhism while in Tibet. The abbot of the Surmang Monasteries and the governor of the Surmang District of Eastern Tibet, Trungpa Rinpoche was forced to flee his homeland in 1959 to escape persecution by the Chinese Communists. His harrowing journey over the Himalayas to freedom lasted ten months.

After several years in India, where he was the spiritual adviser to the Young Lamas School, Rinpoche immigrated to England, where he studied at Oxford University and established the Samye Ling Meditation Centre in Scotland. Following a serious automobile accident in 1969, which he regarded as a message to be more open and courageous, Trungpa Rinpoche gave up his monastic robes and became a lay teacher, in order to communicate more directly with Western students. In January 1970, he married Diana Judith Pybus and shortly thereafter immigrated with her to North America, where he remained until his death in 1987.

One of the first Tibetan lineage holders to present the Buddhist teachings in English, Chögyam Trungpa became one of the most important influences on the development of Buddhism in the West, thanks to his command of the English language and his understanding of Western mind. He established hundreds of meditation centers throughout North America, founded Naropa University in Boulder, Colorado—the first Buddhist-inspired university in North America—and attracted several thousand committed students who received advanced teachings from him and have continued to propagate his teachings and lineage in North America. Chögyam Trungpa was also instrumental in bringing many other great Tibetan lineage holders to teach in North America.

He also established Shambhala Training, a program designed to present meditation and the Shambhala tradition of warriorship to a broad audience. The author of more than two dozen popular books on Buddhism, meditation, and the path of Shambhala warriorship, he was an ecumenical teacher who sought out the wisdom in other schools of Buddhism and in other religions. He also studied and promoted a contemplative awareness of the visual arts, design, poetry, theater, and other aspects of Western art and culture.

Chögyam Trungpa died in 1987, in Halifax, Nova Scotia, at the age of forty-seven. He is survived by his wife and five sons. His eldest son, Sakyong Mipham Rinpoche, succeeds him as the lineage holder and the spiritual head of Shambhala.

Trungpa Rinpoche is widely acknowledged as a pivotal figure in introducing the buddhadharma to the Western world. He joined his great appreciation for Western culture with his deep understanding of his own tradition. This led to a revolutionary approach to teaching the dharma, in which the most ancient and profound teachings were presented in a thoroughly contemporary way. Trungpa Rinpoche is celebrated for his fearless proclamation of the teachings: free from hesitation, true to the purity of the tradition, and utterly fresh.

Index

aggression, 48–49, 80, 122, 123, 124;
    ego and, 45–46; guarding against,
    37–38; overcoming, 22; renuncia-
    tion and, 59–62. *See also* hatred
anger, 59. *See also* aggression
appreciation, 77, 81, 85, 94–95, 112, 115
arrogance, positive, 35–36
Ashe, 100, 101; absolute, 89–90; and
    basic goodness, 87–90; meanings
    of, 83–84; relative, 84–85, 89
assassination, 66–67
awareness, 12–13, 17, 101, 112

balanced state of being, 46–51
basic goodness, 8–10, 55, 120; *Ashe*
    and, 87–90; in conflicts, 60, 61–62;
    expression of, 83–84; fearlessness
    and, 69, 72–73, 122–23; sacred out-
    look and, 57. *See also* unconditional
    goodness
beliefs, wrong, 57–58, 60
bewilderment, 4, 63
body and mind, synchronizing, 75,
    76, 80, 82
Book of Changes (I Ching), 70–71
boredom, 59, 99
bow and arrow analogy, 65–66, 67
bravery, 3, 130; in the art of war, 50;
    cowardice and, 63; goodness and,
    9; simplicity and, 62
breath, 13, 14, 129

brilliance. See *ziji*
Buddha. *See* Shakyamuni Buddha
buddha, heart of, 21
buddha nature, 10, 20, 21–22, 33
Buddhism, 3, 32, 48, 71–72; buddha
    nature in, 10; compassion in, 73;
    emptiness in, 16, 57, 89, 117; renun-
    ciation in, 59; secular experiences
    and, 103; sun and moon symbolism
    in, 25–26; teacher, role of in, 20–21,
    22; vajrayana, 89, 129–30

celebration, 81–82, 88–89
chaos, 97
charisma, 88. See also *ziji*
cheerfulness, 19, 36, 100
cocoon, 39, 41–43
communication, 88, 93–95, 98; genu-
    ine, 104–5; longing for, 119
compassion, 29, 49–50, 73
confidence, 48, 105, 107, 113. *See also*
    primordial confidence; uncondi-
    tional confidence
conflict, relating with, 60–62
confusion, 65, 76, 79
container, 27
cowardice, 37, 82, 104; bravery and, 63;
    facing, 3–4, 102; fear and, 84, 109
cutting through, 84

delight, 41, 81, 99

143

COVER ART

Head of Buddha, ca. 560. China, Northern Qi dynasty (550–577).
Limestone; H. 15 ½ in. (39.4 cm); W. 10 in. (25.4 cm); D. 12 in. (30.5 cm).
Gift of Mr. and Mrs. Albert Roothbert, 1957 (57.176).
The Metropolitan Museum of Art, New York, NY, U.S.A.
Image © The Metropolitan Museum of Art / Art Resource, NY.